THE LAMB, THE BEAS

The Lamb,
the Beast
& the Devil

Making Sense of the Book of Revelation

JOHN HOSIER

MONARCH
BOOKS

Mill Hill, London & Grand Rapids, Michigan

First published by Monarch Books in the UK 2002,
Concorde House, Grenville Place,
Mill Hill, London, NW7 3SA.

Distributed by:
UK: STL, PO Box 300, Kingstown Broadway, Carlisle,
Cumbria CA3 0QS;
USA: Kregel Publications, PO Box 2607
Grand Rapids, Michigan 49501.

ISBN 1 85424 582 1

British Library Cataloguing Data
A catalogue record for this book is available
from the British Library.

Book design and production for the publishers by
Bookprint Creative Services
P.O. Box 827, BN21 3YJ, England.
Printed in Great Britain.

To the Church of Christ the King, Brighton, UK

CONTENTS

FOREWORD

My family and I recently moved to central London. We have begun to familiarize ourselves with the City of Westminster where we live, finding our way around nearby streets and famous landmarks like Westminster Abbey, the Houses of Parliament and Whitehall. But places further afield such as Hackney, Ealing, Islington, Camden and Lewisham seem like visiting another planet. London is so vast that even London cabbies can take up to seven years to acquire what they call "The Knowledge" before they are licensed to drive passengers around without getting them lost!

Of course, there's always the London *A to Z*, but it's printed in such extraordinary detail you can easily miss the wood for the trees! No, what we as a family really need, at this stage, is to be able to see the "Big Picture" at a glance, from a map drawn to a larger scale – the details can come later.

It's a bit like this when you try to find your way through the book of Revelation. You need a reliable guide, so that you won't get lost. You need the "Big Picture". Massive commentaries that explore every single detail, in hundreds of pages of close print, are readily available. They examine every word, every mysterious image, and every Old Testament allusion along with the historical background and every possible alternative interpretation. These works are invaluable, provided you have the stamina to complete them. But many of us just want to find our way around quickly, so that we don't get lost.

In the aftermath of the New York tragedy of September 11th 2001, and the reality of the increasingly unstable world that we all now inhabit, no book in the Bible could be more important for every Christian to become more familiar with than the book of Revelation. This commentary helps us to straddle the huge gap between the 21st century and the strange world of the 1st century with its apocalyptic imagery of candlesticks, trumpets, bowls, horses, rivers, plagues, locusts, dragons and lakes of fire.

John Hosier has written in a very clear style, accessible to all, yet refusing to dodge any of the important issues of interpretation. Because of this, he has done a brilliant bridge-building job in this brief commentary. He enables us to commute between two seemingly unrelated worlds, the world of the Apostle John and our own.

We can return full of hope. And above all we will be enabled to see Christ himself – still glorious, still reigning, still in charge, still in total control and returning soon.

I strongly suspect that this convenient and usable presentation will open up the book of Revelation for many readers in a new way, and spur others to study more deeply because it has served to orientate them correctly. It will certainly give you hope for the future.

Who knows? One great result of reading this book could be that Revelation will become your favourite book in the Bible!

Greg Haslam
Minister, Westminster Chapel, London

INTRODUCTION

There are certain days when we feel that history is being made. During the writing of this book, the terrorist attacks took place in Washington and New York on 11 September 2001. It was immediately being spoken of as a day that would change history. It will take future generations to decide how true that claim proves to be. But history is being made every day in the great and small events that take place in our world. The book of Revelation gives us God's perspective on all that is happening on any day and in any year in history. True, some people will try to suggest that a particular historical event is actually described in Revelation. But such attempts are based on very subjective judgements and will always be challenged by others. However, the book of Revelation does give us the opportunity to see all that happens against the background of God's purposes on the earth. So this book, while making no direct reference to 11 September 2001, will still give us a way of understanding the events of that day and those that have followed.

We live in a world that experiences, among other things, disasters, wars, disease and earthquakes. What sense do we make of all this? Is life and history simply drifting on without any real direction or meaning? While not, I believe, describing any particular event in history that we have yet seen, Revelation nevertheless gives us a clear view of what life is like and, in general terms, what happens across the course of the centuries. We are moving towards the return of Christ, towards a new heaven and earth and towards the eternal age. Revelation tells us of these things and constantly reassures us with the message that in the end all the triumph and the victory are with God in the fulfilment of his plans.

There are excellent and scholarly commentaries available on the book of Revelation. This book is not written as a commentary, though it has drawn heavily on some that are available. It is written in an accessible style with hardly a reference to other works (although it is very dependent upon them). Many Christians avoid the book of Revelation because they either see it as too hard to understand or feel it has been undermined by some rather weird or cranky interpretations. My desire has been to write in such a way that any interested believer can gain a clear, easily understandable overview of Revelation and find it encouraging and faith-building to do so. I enclose a list of commentaries at the end for those who would like to study Revelation in much greater depth and on a verse-by-verse basis.

Ideally, it would be best to read the relevant section of Revelation (most commonly one chapter) before reading each chapter of this book. However, this is not strictly necessary as the sense of each section is given in the chapters of this book and many, though by no means all, the verses are quoted.

Although I have read many different commentaries myself, and I certainly seek to stay within the evangelical parameters of the meaning of Revelation, I am of course responsible for the various interpretations given here.

I would like to thank Wendy Owen and Annie Waller for their patience and help in the initial stages of writing this down and also David Brand for his thorough attention to the detail of the text and his many helpful suggestions.

Sadly, the book of Revelation is too much neglected. I trust this, hopefully, readable and accessible style will contribute to opening up to many more believers the truth that God is absolutely sovereign over all things and, as has been said so often, history is HIS STORY.

CHAPTER ONE

THE TIME IS NEAR
Revelation 1:1–3

Right at the beginning, this book announces itself as the revelation of Jesus Christ. This title immediately gives us a clue to the type of literature that we are reading. The Greek word for "revelation" can also be translated as "apocalypse", which is the title given to this book in some editions of the Bible. For us, the readers of this book, this term conveys some key information.

The style of writing

At first glance, this book comes as something of a shock. We read of seals and trumpets and bowls of wrath. We are given the figures of 144,000 (people) and 1,000 (years). Jerusalem is described as descending from heaven, and we read of a beast arising from the sea. Much seems odd and mysterious. Part of the explanation is that Revelation is apocalyptic literature. Such writing would have been familiar to the book's first readers. It was a style of writing that relied heavily on numbers, symbols and pictures; these were often used to disguise political statements that it might have been dangerous to make in a more open fashion. We have here something rather like a code which needs to be cracked. Often, in the book of Revelation, the meaning is obvious. Sometimes, however, the correct interpretation presents us with more of a challenge.

Apocalyptic writing was also used to predict unknown, but dark, events. However, the book of Revelation, although it includes descriptions of future events, differs from apocalyptic literature generally in not being negative, gloomy and despairing, but positive and victorious.

An apocalypse also refers to a revelation, in the literal sense of an unveiling. During the long reign of our present queen she has had a number of portraits painted. These have always been kept secret until the apocalypse – the day of unveiling. Suddenly, everyone is able to see what was previously hidden, and approving or critical comments can then be made!

Similarly, when we read the book of Revelation an unveiling takes place, and we view what was previously hidden and kept secret. The Bible is God's inspired and "breathed-out" revelation to us. We find here some of the previously hidden secrets and purposes of God.

The revelation of Jesus Christ

The very first phrase of this book raises a technical matter for us. "The revelation of Jesus Christ" (verse 1) – is this "a revelation that Jesus gives", or is it "a revelation about Jesus Christ"? It's a debated point, but I would favour "a revelation about Jesus Christ". So, at the very beginning of the book, there is an announcement. This is "the revelation *about* Jesus Christ". This is a book about him, above every other theme. It is about his supremacy over all the events of history. It is about his return to conclude history. If we want to know what God is doing in history – to understand the course of history, to grasp events at the end of history, or even to probe into eternity – we need a revelation of Jesus Christ. None of these can be understood without a revelation of him.

This is also a revelation that is accessible to us. Verse 1 speaks of God showing his servants what must soon take place. If we are the servants of God, then the revelation is given to us. It was first given to the apostle John by an angel, and then John wrote it down; but because it is a revelation for the servants of God, it is definitely for us. Therefore this is a book that we are intended to understand. Not everything is immediately obvious and simple, but it is accessible. We must not approach it with a kind of hopeless attitude, never expecting to understand, or even believing that we are not really meant to understand it. No, this is a revelation given to the servants of God; we *can* understand it. God is the source of all truth. Man never invents truth; he can only receive it. So this book is a God-given revelation of his truth to us, and it *is* accessible.

Timing

One of the challenges of this book is the timing of events. Verse 1 speaks of what must "soon" take place. In verse 3 we read that "the time is near." Students of Revelation have come up with different ideas on how to view the timing of events. Some would see in it descriptions of the events of the Roman empire in John's time and shortly after – so that would be a reference to past history. This is certainly true of some events, but other episodes that are described are clearly in the future, such as the return of Christ, mentioned even in this first chapter:

> Look, he is coming with the clouds,
> and every eye will see him,
> even those who pierced him;
> and all the peoples of the earth will mourn because of him.
> So shall it be!   (verse 7)

A different view puts all the emphasis on events of the end times. Certainly, there is much about these times in Revelation, but we cannot ignore chapters 2 and 3, which describe real churches in John's own lifetime.

Others would suggest that Revelation gives us a panoramic sweep of the whole of human history and that we can read about literal, historical events in the book. That could be possible, but different people see different events being described in the same passage.

My own approach will be to take the best elements from all the above suggestions! We can certainly see events of John's own day reflected in his writing. But it is a book relevant to every stage of history, and it certainly has insights to convey about the end of history.

But we are still left with the words "soon" and "the time is near". We need to make a few comments about this.

Events will take place "soon" and are "near" in the sense that many things in this book are unfolding all the time. Redemption and rebellion are being worked out in the world today and every day. People today are being saved by the victory of Jesus. Christians in some nations are being persecuted right now. So, this book is relevant for every stage of history – and for us now.

Also, it is important to resist the temptation to use Revelation as a detailed and precise description of all events to come. But we can view *every* event in history in the light of Christ's victory and his certain return.

Again, God does not view time as we do. In 1 Peter 4:7 we read that the end of all things is near, and in 1 John 2:18 that this is the last hour. Peter says, "With the Lord a day is like a thousand years, and a thousand years are like a day" (2 Peter 3:8). We could say that God is on a kind of flexi-time! He simply does not regard time in the same way that we do.

But there is a point to all this; it keeps us spiritually on our toes. If you have ever had an experience when you thought that it really might be your last hour, it tends to sharpen you spiritually. As someone once said to me after experiencing a terrifying thunderstorm while camping in a small tent, "It did wonders for my repentance!"

Blessing

There are seven blessings in this book. The first is here in verse 3

– "Blessed is the one who reads the words of this prophecy." We need to believe that any study of this book is going to bless us.

There is blessing for the one who reads the book. This could refer to the public reading of Scripture, which is how this book would normally have been read in the early centuries of Christian history. We know from the early Christian writer Justin Martyr that church services included readings from the Scriptures, which is hardly a surprise. But we learn that there were also official readers in the congregation, and this underlines the importance of the reading of Scripture.

There is also blessing for those who hear this book being read. This can be understood very literally as one's heart soars on hearing passages that exalt God and declare his majesty and victory.

There is also blessing for those who study this book. As we dig into it, we discover that John really *saw* something. "After this I looked, and there before me was a door standing open in heaven. And the voice I had first heard speaking to me like a trumpet said, 'Come up here and I will show you what must take place after this.'" (4:1). John *sees* the message of God.

This may help to explain some of the difficulties we encounter. John sees mysteries of God revealed. An angel tells John to write it down, and that is quite a challenge. It's difficult enough to describe a snowflake; but John is looking into heaven and seeing the purposes of God unfold. He is given a vision of Jesus returning. How do you write that down?! But he does. So the blessing is for us as we read, listen and study this book.

In verse 2, John says that he testifies to everything he saw. He saw the Word of God. In the first chapter of his gospel, John describes Jesus as the Word of God who became flesh. God's word becomes flesh in us as we obey it rather than merely hearing or reading it, and we always need this to happen. So John emphasizes this by saying that blessing is for those who take to heart what is written in the book. In fact, apart from the letters to the seven churches, Revelation does not tell us to *do* a great deal. But we will be very blessed if we take to heart what *is* written.

We need to keep our focus on the centrality of Christ, keep our confidence in his victory, and remain certain of his return.

All history is moving towards a climax. There are alarming events that take place right through the ages. We need a revelation of Jesus Christ. Do matters sometimes seem out of our control, as mortal men and women? Well, there is a glorified Man in heaven. He is not dead, but alive. There is a Lamb that has been slain, but he stands in the centre of the throne as the resurrected Lord. The seals, which herald great events upon the earth, are being opened. Jesus is assembling his angelic harvesters of humanity. A great white horse will one day ride forth from heaven, bearing the King of kings and Lord of lords. Jesus will be revealed from heaven with mighty angels and great glory to consummate his victory. All creation will one day be utterly transformed. We are going to read about all of this and much more.

This book, the Revelation of Jesus Christ, provides us with an anchor in a storm. It is like sunshine in the gloom. It grounds us on solid rock while everything else trembles and falls. We *can* keep on going, for the time is near!

CHAPTER TWO

THE LORD GOD ALMIGHTY
Revelation 1:4–8

John greets his readers in verse 4 with the use of his own name. John is the writer of this book, but he is not the author; he receives a revelation, and an angel tells him to write it down. John addresses seven churches in Asia Minor, so could that mean that we are not included?

This question brings us to the use of numbers in this book. Many different numbers are used and can be interpreted to mean almost anything. Some have suggested that the number 7 should be understood as 3 + 4, which is the number of the Trinity plus the gospels. But why should it be understood like that? Actually, 7 is one of the safest numbers to interpret in this book. It has always been understood as God's perfect number, representing completeness. A week is seven days, reflecting the six days of creation, together with the seventh day on which God rested. The number 7 seems to be part of the natural rhythm of life. We find this number 54 times in this book. Some would even suggest that the book itself naturally falls into seven parts, a claim that I would resist as being a rather forced division of the text, but it does illustrate the predominance of the number 7.

These seven churches were real, living churches situated in the Roman province of Asia Minor. But there were far more than seven churches there, so why are these particular seven singled out? It could simply be that Jesus had a message only for these seven churches. But there is another possibility. These seven churches could at the same time represent the complete church of Jesus Christ. In fact, as we study the seven letters we find that they are also relevant for us today, as indeed they have been for the church throughout the centuries of Christian history. So, far from any idea of us being excluded, we are probably talking of something totally inclusive: the whole church of Jesus Christ.

There is a typical but not stereotyped greeting in the phrase, "Grace and peace to you" (verse 4). Grace denotes a power: the operation of the Spirit in the life of the believer so that he might enjoy the benefits of salvation. "Grace to you" means "May you know the power of God working in your life, so that all the benefits of being saved by Christ are real in your experience", and therefore we always need this grace. This "grace" is linked with "peace" because the fruit of such grace in our lives is peace with God (Romans 5:1–2).

We are told about the source of this grace: the Triune God. The language here is so rich about God: he who is, he who was, and he who is to come. This helps us to recognize the eternal nature and character of God. To Moses, God reveals himself as **I AM**. God simply **IS** and therefore he was (always) and he will be (always).

When we try to think of God as eternal, it can send us dizzy because we are restricted by a sense of time. We can look up at the sky and out at the stars and feel quite giddy, for they were created so long ago and are so incredibly far away. But for all their age, they were created at some time, and the distance of every one of them is finite. There was a time when they were not, but God eternally **IS**. Everything in the universe is caused by something else. But ultimately, there is God. What caused God? Nothing and no one, for God always **IS**. He is self-existent and infinite; he is the uncaused Cause, and he is the source of grace to you and me.

Who are the seven spirits before the throne of God? (verse 4)

This is the first real puzzle in this book and causes some speculation. However, everyone sees it as some kind of reference to the
Holy Spirit. The number 7 is used and so we may best understand this as a reference to the full number of blessings and to the
fullness of the Holy Spirit in the life of every believer. We cannot
over-define the work of the Holy Spirit. Therefore we may need
to be content with what may be more of an impression rather
than a perfect explanation of this phrase. What is conveyed is a
sense of the Holy Spirit's fullness and blessing.

Then we have a reference to Jesus Christ and to three particular truths about him (verse 5).

He is a faithful witness

Jesus tells us and shows us what God is like. In Hebrews 1:3 we
read, "The Son is the radiance of God's glory and the exact representation of his being." Jesus told Philip that anyone who had
seen him had seen the Father (John 14:9).

He is the firstborn from the dead

This is an important statement and ought to be compared with
Colossians 1:15: "He is the image of the invisible God, the firstborn over all creation." To understand this as meaning that Christ
was created in time, as some of the cults have suggested, actually
speaks of an ignorance of the wider teaching of the Bible. In
Jeremiah 31:9 we read of "Ephraim . . . my firstborn son". In
fact, Joseph's son Manasseh was born before Ephraim. However,
Joseph's father, Jacob, gave the greater blessing to Ephraim and
he was to come to greater prominence. Sometimes Israel is
referred to as the "firstborn" nation, which it was not in terms of
time, but the reference is to its prominence in the purposes of
God. Similarly, when we read that Jesus is the firstborn over all
creation, there is an acknowledgement that he is the Sovereign
Lord; that he is pre-eminent.

More than that, Jesus is the firstborn from the dead. You could point out that others rose from the dead before Jesus did. But none was more prominent. And while others were resurrected back to this life, Jesus was raised to eternal life.

He is ruler of the kings of the earth

We know that this is a messianic prophecy, based on Psalm 89:27. The original readers of Revelation, and Christians throughout history, all know that, though the kings of the earth (the worldly authorities) may flex their muscles and move against the church, Jesus remains the one who is King of kings and ruler of the kings of the earth. Christians today also know the same truth: Jesus is Lord.

This is some greeting and some greeter!

Response and adoration

This book of Revelation will always motivate us to worship. There is strong meat here for our worship – it isn't simply, "Whistle a happy tune." We are stirred to adoration and praise by a revelation of Jesus and what he has done. There are some compelling reasons given for this in verses 5 and 6.

He loves us

The text literally speaks of "him who loves us". Because of the eternal nature of Jesus, there is an eternal element to his loving us. It began in eternity, before time, when he chose us for himself. It has been demonstrated in time when, in human flesh, Jesus descended to experience suffering and death for us. It continues in the present time and at every moment of the future, for nothing "will be able to separate us from the love of God" (Romans 8:39). It will continue in eternity beyond time because he will love us for ever.

I am aware that to speak of God loving us can just sound like words from a thousand sermons, particularly when we speak of God's active love for us now. Certainly, God has loved us, for he saved us. But how do I know that he really loves me now? We can go to a Sunday service and hear the same words again and again – "God loves you" – but where are the demonstrations of God's love for me now? We can sometimes think, "I'm sick of the words: show me some evidence!" The reasons we are tempted to doubt the present love of God (though still believing in the saving love of God) are the pressures and problems of life. They seem to be evidence that God is not actively showing his love, otherwise, why would I face these things? Well, whoever suggested that the Christian life would set us free from present troubles? Not Jesus: "In this world you will have trouble" (John 16:33) is a very definite statement. Trouble is guaranteed. But that doesn't mean Jesus doesn't love us now: everything we do, even every breath that we draw, is by his grace. The one whom we adore is the one who eternally loves us.

He freed us from our sins by his blood

This is another reason for our adoration of Jesus. When God sets free, he sets free by blood. When Moses led the Hebrews out of slavery in Egypt, they were delivered by blood. The blood of the lamb was on their doorposts, and it guaranteed to them security and deliverance. The Egyptians, with no blood on their doorposts, suffered the death of each family's firstborn child. The blood of the lamb brought protection, but it was also the mark of deliverance for God's people, for the plague of death in Egypt resulted in the Hebrews' expulsion from the land. The exodus began; the people of God were delivered.

Because of the blood of Jesus, we are involved in a new exodus. We are delivered from slavery and death. One payment has been sufficient to free us from guilt and shame and condemnation. That payment has been the life and death of the Son of God. With the shedding of blood he sets us free from our sin.

> He breaks the power of cancelled sin,
> He sets the prisoner free;
> His blood can make the foulest clean;
> His blood availed for me.'

– Charles Wesley

Freed from sin by one, decisive act – this says everything we need to hear to cause us to worship Jesus.

He made us to be a kingdom of priests

God intended the nation of Israel to be a kingdom of priests: "Although the whole earth is mine, you will be for me a kingdom of priests and a holy nation" (Exodus19:5–6).

That is what we are to understand here in Revelation, and it is emphasized in 1 Peter 2:9: ". . . you are a chosen people, a royal priesthood." How does this work? I live in the city of Brighton on the south coast of England. I could catch a train to Victoria Station in London, walk to Buckingham Palace and say to the soldier at the gate, "I am a loyal subject of the queen and I would like her to answer a request of mine." I could then walk across the forecourt of the palace and, speaking to a policeman at the door, could say, "I am a loyal subject of the queen and I would like her to answer a request of mine." Entering the palace, I could then search from room to room until, finding the queen sitting on a throne, I could say, "I am a loyal subject of Your Majesty and I would like you to answer my request." Would I be able to do this? Not a chance! But today, because God has made us priests, we can go directly to the King of kings and Lord of lords and ask him to grant us our request. Wonderful!

Future grace

This is the title given by John Piper to one of his books. Here in Revelation chapter 1 we read of the grace of God coming in the future. Here is a brief introduction to the return of Jesus – a subject that will occupy us several times in this book. Verse 7 tells us to pay attention, to be alert! Look, Jesus is coming back with the clouds of glory! There is some brief detail at this point. Every eye will see him. Those who have pierced him will see him. We can understand that absolutely literally, for the Bible teaches that when Jesus returns there will be a resurrection of the wicked and the righteous (John 5:29). All peoples of the earth will mourn. As we take the Bible as a whole, we see that there will be believers from every people group who will rejoice at Christ's return. But the unbelieving peoples of the earth will mourn to see a King who can never be their Saviour.

What an amazing, sobering, awesome moment that will be! John says, "So shall it be" (verse 7). It will most definitely happen. There is one thing we can be certain of concerning future events in this world: Jesus is coming with the clouds of glory. Nothing will prevent that. There is no alternative plan. There is no vagueness here. More than 300 times, the Bible tells us that that day will come. Every people group will receive the gospel. The full number of the Gentiles will come in. "All Israel will be saved" (Romans 11:26), referring to a mighty turning of the Jewish nation to Jesus. The world will hear the trumpet of God and the shout of the archangel. The King will return. **So shall it be**.

For us who believe, it is future grace. God's amazing grace will come to us in the future with the return of Jesus. History as we know it, and the world as we know it, will come to an end on that day. There will be an ending and an eternal beginning.

This section ends with another strong declaration: "'I am the Alpha and the Omega,' says the Lord God, 'who is, and who was, and who is to come, the Almighty'"(verse 8). Alpha and omega are the first and last letters of the Greek alphabet. They refer to the beginning and the end. They are therefore parallel to the description of God as the one who was and is to come. Again, this refers to God's eternal existence. This is what God is: eternal, the beginning and the end. And of course, if God always was and always will be, then it follows that he always **is**.

This undeniable description of the Lord God's eternal existence needs to be understood by those who believe that Jesus was in fact created at some infinitely distant time in the past. These people teach that Jesus is not God but a lesser god. However, if we go to Revelation 22:13, we see Jesus described also as "the Alpha and the Omega . . . the Beginning and the End". It is the same description that is given to God. God the Father and God the Son, together with God the Holy Spirit, are co-equal and co-eternal.

The Greek word for "almighty" is "pantocrator", which is carried across into English. The dictionaries define "pantocrator" as "ruler of the universe". It is a powerful word, used seven times in the New Testament. It occurs six times in Revelation and also in 2 Corinthians 6:18. For the early Christians, to know that God was Pantocrator when they were facing persecution, meeting in little scattered groups across an empire that was ruled with military might and controlled by an emperor from Rome, would have been more than just a nice devotional thought. Ultimately, God really *is* in charge!

In the Roman empire there were hundreds of thousands of slaves. Many came to Christ, but they still had to live under the yoke of Roman oppression. They were already treated as things rather than people, and, as Christians, were now vulnerable to even more hatred and brutality. But to these redeemed people comes this mighty declaration, "I am the Alpha and the Omega . . . who is, and who was, and who is to come, the [Pantocrator]." This ruler does not control a passing empire – he rules the universe for ever.

This is an important truth for us today. We may feel pushed around by other people and vulnerable to their criticisms of our faith. But we submit and belong to the eternal one. He is our King, the Lord God Almighty, the Pantocrator, the ruler of the universe. As such, he is always worthy of our response and adoration.

CHAPTER THREE

THE GLORY OF CHRIST
Revelation 1:9–20

John, the writer of Revelation, has already been mentioned in verse 4, but now he makes a more personal introduction in verse 9. The early Christian writer Eusebius tells us that there were twelve apostles, and that all of them were martyred for their faith except John.

In old age, at a time of persecution for the church, he was sent into exile to the island of Patmos, but returned to die in Ephesus. John speaks of himself as being on the island of Patmos "because of the word of God and the testimony of Jesus". This probably refers to his own faithful preaching and witness to the gospel.

On Patmos, John is first of all our brother. This man was an outstanding apostle, one of the original twelve, and is described as the one whom Jesus loved. But he is still simply the brother of every Christian. Churches need strong leaders, with a sense of vision and purpose. The ascended Christ has always been giving to the church: apostles, prophets, evangelists, pastors and teachers. But none of these are any more saved than the rest of us. We are all brothers and sisters in Christ.

John is also a "companion in the suffering and kingdom and patient endurance" (verse 9). "Suffering" which can also be translated as "tribulation", has the root meaning of pressure. The idea is of fruit in a press with the juice being squeezed out. If we are in trouble, or under pressure, or feeling squeezed out, then we have a companion: the apostle John.

The word "tribulation" here comes in as a trailer to "the great tribulation" that we will look at in later chapters. To some extent, the church is always going through tribulation, though it is worse at some times and in some places than in others. We have already seen that Jesus promised his followers trouble in this world. I sometimes say that we are promised two things as Christians – eternal life and a rough ride! Acts 14:22 tells us that we must go through many tribulations to enter the kingdom of God. Notice the link there again between tribulation and kingdom. To live under the rule of God (the kingdom dimension) means that we cannot at times avoid living under pressure. What is needed from us at such times? John's answer is: patient endurance. Without faith, troubles simply wear us out. With faith and patient endurance, we inherit what God has promised (Hebrews 6:12). God is therefore doing something great with our characters in times of pressure.

John's vision opens up on the Lord's Day (verse 10). This is the first reference anywhere to this term; the next comes in what is probably the earliest Christian document outside the New Testament, known as the Didache. There are possible alternatives, but the most favoured interpretation is that the Lord's Day is a Sunday. In the time of the early church, when Caesar was worshipped as a god, there were certain parts of the empire where the citizens celebrated "Emperor's Day" once a month. Christians, worshipping the one true God, the Lord who rose on the first day of the week, would celebrate on the Lord's Day every week.

What does it mean for John to claim that he was "in the Spirit" on the Lord's Day (verse 10)? We see this kind of experience in the life of Ezekiel (Ezekiel 3:12) and in the life of the apostle Paul, when he describes himself as caught up to the third heaven and hearing things which he is not even permitted to tell (2 Corinthians 12:2–4). There is a dimension of life in the Spirit that should whet our appetite for greater experiences for ourselves.

John is told to write to seven churches, which we will look at in the next chapter, and then he turns to see the voice that was speaking to him (verse 12). It is difficult to see a voice! But I find, at nearly every Christian meeting that I attend, that whenever there is any vocal contribution it causes great curiosity, and members of the congregation turn their heads to see the voice! Perhaps without straining the text too much, we could see here an encouragement to turn whenever we hear the voice of God, and not to remain stiff-necked in disobedience.

The glory of Christ

At this point, the focus is on the one among the seven golden lampstands, which is clearly a vision of Christ in glory (verses 13–16). This is the only really detailed description of Christ's appearance that is given in the New Testament. It is therefore important at that level alone. The gospels, for all their focus on Jesus, give no description, no hint even, of what Jesus looked like as a boy or a man. We have no accurate statues or paintings representing Jesus; all those that we do have are drawn from the imagination of the artist. Clearly, this is God's deliberate plan. Any authentic statue or picture would itself become an object of worship. I incline to the view that, with the exception of his eyes, there was nothing remarkable about the earthly appearance of Jesus. Isaiah states prophetically, "He had no beauty or majesty to attract us to him, nothing in his appearance that we should desire him." (Isaiah 53:2). He was a Saviour, not a film star.

The New Testament accounts of the post-resurrection appearances of Jesus seem to present him differently from time to time. He prepares breakfast on the beach for his disciples, apparently appearing like an ordinary man. In Revelation chapter 1, the appearance of Jesus is one of great glory. In Revelation 5, where he appears as a slain Lamb, it is different again. How do we resolve these apparent variations in the appearance of the risen Jesus?

It may be that they allow us to see and understand Jesus from different points of view. He is a resurrected man. He is also the Lord Jesus Christ exalted in glory. Again, seeing him as a Lamb that was slain reminds us that he is our eternal Redeemer. Jesus' appearance may vary to our view, but that is only in order to help us see the different aspects of truth about him. But here, in the only detailed description of his appearance, we see the glory of Christ.

John draws heavily on Old Testament images, particularly those from the book of Daniel. The manner of his description is most interesting, because he keeps using the word "like". It is as though John is saying, "This is the best I can do; he looked *like* this."

So he is *like* a "son of man". This was Jesus' own term for himself in the gospels. John probably used it to make clear that, though this is Christ in glory, he still resembles a man.

He is dressed in a long robe with a golden sash around his chest. Three types of people in the Old Testament approximate to that description: the angelic messenger who visited Daniel; the priests; and also royalty. This description, then, represents Jesus as prophet, priest and king.

His head and hair are white like wool and snow. Reading Daniel 7:9, we can see this as a symbol of deity. Here is a picture of the God of the ages who acts as judge over the whole world.

His eyes are like blazing fire. What do those eyes express and see? From the gospels, we can detect in the eyes of Jesus the blaze of righteous anger, and the penetration of discernment. Perhaps most poignantly we read in Luke 22:61, "The Lord turned and looked straight at Peter." Nothing is hidden from those penetrating eyes.

He has feet like glowing bronze. This word, used only in Revelation, could describe a gold and silver compound, which would have had a scintillating quality. It has also been described as a mixed metal of great brilliance. Those are the feet to crush every enemy.

His voice was like the sound of rushing waters. "I saw the glory of the God of Israel coming from the east. His voice was like the roar of rushing waters and the land was radiant with his glory" (Ezekiel 43:2). There can be tremendous power and authority in a voice. Imagine hearing the voice of God!

We will return to the seven stars in his right hand. But out of his mouth came a double-edged sword. Similar expressions in the Old Testament as well as in the book of Revelation itself suggest that this is a symbol of the authority of God's word, operating in divine judgement.

Finally, his face shines like the sun. This needs to be compared with what John saw many years earlier on the mount of transfiguration (Luke 9:28–36). At that time, John only glimpsed what he sees more fully here. To see the glory of Christ is to see the one whose face shines like the sun, with dazzling brilliance.

What happens when you are confronted with the glory of God? John falls at his feet as though dead. This seems entirely appropriate and in common with the behaviour of others in the Bible, for example, Daniel 10:7 and Joshua 5:14.

Helen Roseveare, a missionary to the Congo who saw revival there midway through the last century, tells this story:

> I remember one time I was visiting the sick wife of one of the evangelists. I was driving through a dirt track and came to the top of a hill and then suddenly saw this forest fire.
>
> The fire was at the village where we were going and lit up the whole sky. We walked the last few miles but as we got closer I was struck that there was no noise! That was strange. Forest fires have an enormous roar, louder than a plane.
>
> As we got closer, there was also no heat! As we entered the village, one house was ablaze which was the pastor's house – but there were no people about. Again that was strange because everyone would have been out to beat the fire.
>
> Suddenly, there was this terrifying sense of awe. We went into the "blazing" house with flames everywhere but nothing was burned.
>
> The people inside were praising the Lord as the pastor's wife had died and gone to be with Jesus. The Shekinah glory had truly come down upon them.

We are living in days when much is being said about revival.

True revival confronts us with the glory of God. Men fall as though dead. We could do with such glory in the church today.

What happens next?

The Lord tells John not to be afraid, which is enough to raise anyone's suspicions! But to this extraordinary vision John has had of Christ in glory, there are now added three mighty declarations (verses 17–18).

"I am the First and the Last"

This is a clear claim to be divine. We have already seen in verse 8 that God alone is the first and the last. Jesus is making the same claim. Jesus is God. The glory that John has seen is the glory of God.

"I am the Living One"

Christ is eternally alive. The miracle of God made flesh in Christ is that he can say, "I was dead." The eternal one died for us, but that death was followed by resurrection. "I am alive for ever and ever!" It could not be said more strongly. The one who was dead now lives. No other leader can make that claim. Buddha is dead. Muhammad is dead. Hindu gods were never alive. Jesus was dead, but the tomb is empty. No corpse has ever been discovered. Therefore this living one can declare, "I am alive for ever and ever!"

"I hold the keys of death and Hades"

Hades was understood to be the place of the departed dead. But Jesus has power over death and the realm of death into which all men must pass.

For the believer, this knowledge of Christ's lordship helps to remove the fear from death. Its terrors were broken at Calvary. At his return, death itself will die, so that, at the end of Revelation, we read that there will be no more death. Christ is sovereign over death, as Paul reminds us, "If we live, we live to the Lord; and if we die, we die to the Lord. So, whether we live or die, we belong to the Lord" (Romans 14:8).

The church

We have already seen in verses 12 and 13 that Christ is among the seven golden lampstands. We see from verse 20 that these lampstands represent the seven churches to which John has been instructed to write. If we see the number 7 as representing completeness, and the lampstands as symbolizing the churches, we can understand this as Christ standing in the midst of his entire church; the church gathers around Jesus.

Why should these lampstands symbolize the church? We know from the Old Testament that candlesticks stood in the Holy Place. Also, a vision was given to Zechariah of a gold lampstand on which burned seven lights. This was to represent the nation of Israel as the light of God shining in a dark world. Jesus said to his followers, "You are the light of the world" (Matthew 5:14). As churches, we are to shine in the gloom of the world, and we can do so with Christ in our midst.

There are two other sevens. In verse 20 we meet the seven angels of the seven churches. Who are these angels? Some say that they are the elders of the churches; others have said that they are the guardian angels of the churches, and there are other interpretations as well. The matter is not ultimately of great importance, for clearly the letters are directed to these seven churches and meant to be read to them.

The seven stars are spoken of as the seven angels (verse 20); yet in verse 16, where we read that Christ holds these seven stars in his right hand, the most natural way to understand them would again be as a picture of the church that Christ holds securely.

The church may be persecuted and under great pressure. But it is not Caesar or any earthly leader who is sovereign; the destiny of the church is not at the disposal of any worldly powers. Rather, the ever-living Christ is sovereign, and he holds the church securely in his hand.

CHAPTER FOUR

HOPE FOR WEARY AND LUKEWARM CHURCHES
Revelation 2 and 3

The letters to the seven churches are often thought of as the easy part of Revelation. Many series of sermons are preached on Revelation 2 and 3, even if the rest of the book is avoided. I will give a brief overview of the seven letters, and then in the rest of this chapter we will look at the first and the last of these letters.

Some have suggested that these seven churches represent the seven ages of church history. Not only is that difficult to fit in with Scripture as a whole, but it does also seem to be an entirely subjective viewpoint. Who decides which age corresponds to each church? Why is it that churches today are always put in the Laodicean age? The church at Laodicea is infamous for being lukewarm. But it is not true to say that today the entire church worldwide is lukewarm. In some places it is burning hot. On the other hand, throughout church history there have always been individual churches that at times were lukewarm. This should give us a clue to the correct interpretation here. These seven churches face just the same kinds of pressure, and exhibit just the same kinds of strength and weakness, that local churches have shown in every age of church history. What we have in these seven churches are challenges and warnings that are relevant for every church in every age. "Taken in general, the church always presents this seven-fold aspect, and appears with a mixture of light and darkness, good and evil qualities, attractive and repulsive features." (H. Hoeksema, *Behold He Cometh*, p. 138)

Three of these seven churches were troubled by false teachers: those at Ephesus, Pergamum and Thyatira. Two of the churches were harassed by persecution: those at Smyrna and Philadelphia. The churches at Sardis and Laodicea both showed signs of spiritual poverty.

The church in Ephesus

Ephesus was a city of great political importance. Rome had granted it a measure of self-government within the empire, with its own democratically elected authority. The athletic games that were held there were second only in importance to the Olympic Games.

At the time that John was writing, we know that Ephesus was a great commercial centre. In the days of the Roman empire, trade ran along rivers and roads. Ephesus had both. It stood at the mouth of a river and was also a great seaport (now silted up). There were also three great roads that converged on Ephesus: one brought trade from the east, one brought trade from Asia Minor and the other brought trade from the south. This was a prosperous, cosmopolitan and busy city.

Most significantly, it was a city of great religious importance. The greatest glory of Ephesus was the temple of Diana (or in Greek, Artemis). In the time of the New Testament this temple was one of the seven wonders of the world. There was a Greek saying: "The sun sees nothing finer in his course than Diana's temple." When it was built, many of the wealthy women of the city gave up their jewellery for its decoration. Alexander the Great offered all the spoils of his Eastern campaign to have his name inscribed on the temple – and was refused. Only the name of Diana could be associated with it.

It was a magnificent construction, with 127 marble pillars, each the gift of a king. The image of Diana was hidden by a black velvet curtain behind the temple altar. This idol has been described as black, squat, many-breasted and repulsive. It symbolized fertility and drew the worship of multitudes. The worship of Diana was trance-like and frenzied, and would culminate in gross immorality through the service of the temple priestesses, who in reality were prostitutes.

To this extraordinary city came the apostle Paul, who, in a three-year period, probably enjoyed the most effective phase of his whole ministry here. Every day in the lecture hall of Tyrannus he would declare the gospel, so that we read in Acts that all the Gentiles and Jews in the province of Asia heard the word of the Lord. This would be a reference to the many merchants and traders who would have heard Paul preach as they passed through this great city.

Some historians say that the church in Ephesus grew to 30,000 and others even to 60,000 members. At the end of the first century it was probably the most important church in the world. Paul, Timothy, the apostle John and Mary, the mother of Jesus, all seem to have been associated with this church.

The church at Ephesus is one commended by Jesus for not growing weary. In our age there is plenty to cause church members to feel weary. There is the pace of life, the strain of maintaining good relationships, the challenge of materialism, with massive enticements to give all our time to making more money. There are also the genuine hardships, disappointments, or hurts that come into people's lives.

This letter suggests ways we can resist weariness:

Remember

Although the church at Ephesus is commended for not growing weary, it faces the charge of having lost its first love (2:4). I believe that there is a link between these two. If you lose your first love, you are likely to become weary and lose heart. That may not happen for a time, because you can keep to a routine through habit. But eventually, if you forsake your first love, you will become weary. Jesus is really concerned for this church. It is surprising to discover how much discussion there is of the phrase "first love". My suggestion would be that we should understand this loss as a gradual pulling away from a zealous expression of love for Christ. If we forsake such a passion, eventually we will grow weary and lose heart, as disappointments, the snare of materialism and other distractions begin to kick in and take their toll.

Therefore the call is to remember (verse 5) the height from which they have fallen. This height would be their zealous expression of love for Christ. Forsake such a passionate love, and although we may continue with Christian activity for some time, our spiritual life will become empty and hollow. There comes a point where we will say, "What's the point? I've tried and I'm disappointed and hurt. So why keep going?" The only clear remedy is not to forsake our first love. The Christian life should be a love affair between Jesus and ourselves; if it falls short of that, weariness will set in.

It is easy to view a church simply as an organization, but actually it is the gathering together and shepherding of a people devoted to Jesus, in order to help them express that devotion. In Hebrews (12:2) we are told to fix our eyes on Jesus, who for the joy set before him endured the cross. That joy was most certainly us, for beyond the cross Jesus would know the joy of having his own people purchased by his blood. Hebrews 12 goes on to tell us to consider how Jesus endured opposition from sinful men, so that we do not grow weary and lose heart. What drew our love to Jesus first of all was surely his love for us. So, when we feel that we are growing weary in the Christian life, losing heart, or thinking of giving up, we need to ask ourselves what we are considering. We can consider our disappointments, our hurts, or our needs, but what we most need to consider is Jesus Christ and his great love for us.

Repent

If we have been growing weary because of considering the wrong thing, there is a need for repentance.

Do

Do express with passion your love for Jesus. We can do this by pouring out our devotion to him in worship, by loving the saints and by being genuinely concerned for our neighbours.

We will not look at all seven churches in detail, but, having looked at Ephesus, the first in the list, we now look at Laodicea, the last.

The church in Laodicea

The city of Laodicea was founded by Antiochus, who came from the royal family of Syria, in about 250 BC. It was named after his wife.

Three of the most important roads in Asia ran through this city, including a direct link to Ephesus. It was originally constructed as a military fortress, but was always handicapped for that purpose by a lack of water. An aqueduct was constructed carrying water to the city from springs some six miles away. Under Roman rule it had become a most distinguished city by the end of the first century AD. Certain well-known features of Laodicea are clearly reflected in the letter.

It was a prosperous business centre

Laodicea was one of the wealthiest cities in the world. It had a large population of rich and influential Jews. Around 61 AD there was a devastating earthquake in the region; although every other city in the area required government funding to rebuild, Laodicea refused any outside help and was reconstructed from her own resources.

It was a fashion centre

Profitable use was made of local sheep that grew soft, glossy wool. From this wool many garments were manufactured and exported around the empire. This was a city of designer labels and chic fashions!

It was a great medical centre

This feature made the city famous throughout the world. An ointment was produced in Laodicea that helped to cure eye diseases
and give healthy sight.

Who sent the letter?

We know that all of these seven letters came from the risen Christ,
and each of them begins with, "These are the words of . . .",
followed by a description of some aspect of Jesus. There are
three descriptions given of him in this letter (verse 14).

He is "the Amen"

In Isaiah 65:16 we read of the God of truth, literally the God of
"amen". This corresponds to John 3:3, "I tell you the truth . . ." It
could be translated, "Amen, amen", or "Truthfully, truthfully".

Jesus is the truth and therefore he tells the truth. At the end of
someone else's prayer request, we tend to say, "Amen". Why do
we not say, "Yes, please"? – that would have some logic to it!
But "Amen" means "That is the truth", and so is entirely appropriate at the end of a prayer.

He is the faithful and true witness

We say again that Jesus is the truth, and so all that comes from
him is truth. As a witness, Jesus tells us the truth about God, for
he is the truth of God in person.

He is the ruler of God's creation

In Hebrews 1:3 we read that he sustains all things by his powerful word. We have already seen in chapter 1 of Revelation that he
is Pantocrator, the Lord Almighty, the ruler of everything. Here,
that is confirmed once again.

In Ephesians 3:8 Paul speaks of the unsearchable riches of
Christ. This is perhaps best understood as the infinite riches of
Christ. You can search them out, but they are inexhaustible. No

matter how much we keep looking at Christ, there is always more to say about him. He is the truth. He is an utterly reliable witness. He is the ruler of creation, and we could go on indefinitely. And this Christ is the author of the letter.

What does he say?

Jesus has nothing good to say about this church. Rather, there is disapproval and accusation. This church is lukewarm. The church at Laodicea is infamous for this criticism, but the word "lukewarm" is deliberate, and would have been full of meaning to the members of that church. Opposite the city a mineral stream could be seen tumbling over a cliff. It was rich in lime, and although hot as it spilled over the cliff, by the time it had passed through a series of pools the water was tepid and lukewarm. It made a nauseating drink. We can easily understand that a hot cup of tea or a drink from an ice-cold mountain stream would be much better. But what does this mean spiritually? For if you take the words literally they do not make complete sense. Surely, in a spiritual sense, lukewarm must be better than freezing cold. True, it would be better still to be boiling hot. Yet Jesus rejects that which is lukewarm.

At this point we need to remember that we are reading apocalyptic literature, and that there could be some hidden meaning here. Really, the emphasis is on the fact that this church makes Jesus feel sick, just as we would feel if we drank chemically-rich, tepid water. *The Message* translates this graphically as: "You make me want to vomit." That is the issue, and it is put starkly and dramatically.

We can use the word "awesome" rather casually sometimes, but it is awesome to realize that Jesus knows everything about our church, and we might wonder what he thinks of it! We know that he loves us – he has purchased us, we are his people and his body, and one day we will be his bride. Jesus would never disown us, but what does he think of our spiritual condition? Certainly, he would be able to say of our church, "I know your

deeds." Over the years, I have met some people who have tried
to guess what Jesus thinks of a particular church. What they are
really telling me is what *they* think of that church!

But if this letter to Laodicea has relevance to every church in
every age, then there will be some warnings here for us. Why did
this church make Jesus feel sick? "You say, 'I am rich; I have
acquired wealth and do not need a thing.' But you do not realize
that you are wretched, pitiful, poor, blind and naked" (verse 17).
Of course, this was something that was literally true, since the
church reflected the spirit of the city of Laodicea, a spirit of independence and self-sufficiency; the smug satisfaction of a people
who believe they can achieve whatever they want to, and do not
include God in the picture. What could indicate such an attitude
in the church today?

There can be three aspects of our life that indicate that we do
have an attitude like this; they are:

Prayerlessness

This is the idea that we can build our church and run our own
lives, and that we are too busy to pray. What we are actually saying is that we do not need God.

Sinfulness

We can take the view that there is no clear evidence that God
takes an interest in what we do, or indeed that he even sees what
we are doing. We can get away with things, and on the whole we
seem to. Sinfulness can be expressed in an attitude that says that
we do not need the blessing of God. It is then convenient to call
holiness legalism as our excuse for what we do.

Casualness

Being "laid back" and "cool" are favourite postures for today. If
schoolchildren work too enthusiastically they may be told to
"cool it" by their classmates. It is not cool to be enthusiastic,
especially about God. Self-sufficiency can muzzle our passion
for God. What sickened Jesus was an independent and self-

sufficient spirit. Some churches may look good, but Jesus may bring in the verdict of "wretched, pitiful, poor, blind and naked."

Advice

So how can we break free of a spirit of independence? "I counsel you to buy from me gold refined in the fire, so that you can become rich; and white clothes to wear, so that you can cover your shameful nakedness; and salve to put on your eyes, so that you can see" (verse 18). The Laodiceans would have been able to identify with this. They were materially wealthy, but lacked spiritual riches. They were resplendent in the latest fashions, but were spiritually naked. Nakedness refers to absolute shame. They had their famous ointment for healthy eyes, but were spiritually blind. All of this sounds extraordinarily modern to us, who live in a society obsessed by wealth, health and appearance. This letter speaks to those who feel that they have got it together in those areas of their lives. They are able to live independently of God, but in reality they are in spiritual poverty.

The advice of Jesus is that we should buy spiritual riches from him, to purchase his clothes of righteousness to cover our nakedness and shame. Also, that we should use his ointment for clear spiritual eyesight. But how can we buy those things that can only be obtained freely by grace? Once again, there is a code here to be cracked. In order to enjoy the blessings of God, we require faith. This is the exact opposite of independence, for with faith, we give up on ourselves and trust in Christ alone.

It can often be overlooked that Christ does love this church. "Those whom I love I rebuke and discipline. So be earnest, and repent" (verse 19). Sometimes this letter is read as if the church at Laodicea was being totally rejected. But this is not the case at all, for though her independent spirit makes Jesus sick, he is not rejecting her. Because he loves this church he rebukes her faults; he exercises discipline because he wants her to get rid of her independent spirit. But there is also a glorious promise: "Here I am! I stand at the door and knock. If anyone hears my voice and opens the door, I will come in and eat with him, and he with me" (verse 20). This is often used in an evangelistic sense, but Jesus does not say that he is standing at the door of our heart; rather he is standing at the door of the church. "The only cure for luke-warmness is the readmission of the excluded Christ" (Campbell Morgan). Jesus wants to respond to passionate churches and enjoy fellowship with them.

Assurance

A strong theme in the seven letters is that of rewards for over-comers. For those believers who have been obedient, faithful and persevering, there is the promise of reward. "To him who over-comes, I will give the right to sit with me on my throne, just as I overcame and sat down with my Father on his throne" (verse 21).

As believers, we are already in an elevated position in what Paul describes in Ephesians as "seated . . . with [Christ] in the heavenly realms" (Ephesians 2:6). In the letter to the Laodiceans there is an extra reward, which is to sit with Christ on his throne, "just as I overcame and sat down with my Father on his throne" (verse 21). This promise comes from the risen and exalted Christ to overcomers. Its symbolism is obvious, but it promises us great reward in the future if we persevere.

Appeal

The last letter typically ends with the words, "He who has an ear, let him hear what the Spirit says to the churches" (verse 22). Those churches needed to hear what the Spirit was saying to them, and we too need to hear what the Spirit is saying to our own church.

CHAPTER FIVE

AN OPEN HEAVEN
Revelation 4

Probably no section of the book of Revelation is more helpful to us in the worship of God than the wonderful description we have of an open heaven in chapters 4 and 5.

We have already said that a crucial issue in interpreting Revelation is how we understand the timing of events. The most straightforward way here would seem to be the best way. John has received a vision of Christ in glory. After the letters to the seven churches the vision now continues. Jesus (the one whose voice is like a trumpet) tells John that he is going to give him a revelation about the future. So "what must take place after this" (verse 1) would simply refer to the time from then on.

In this book we are going to see the reality of evil as Satan seeks to extend his kingdom in this world. But we will also see his final and utter defeat. We will read of the establishment of Christ's kingdom and his final and utter victory. But all this is in the future from where John now stands.

Some have suggested that from this point on in the book of Revelation, we are reading of events in heaven and on the earth during the great tribulation, after the church has been raptured and taken from the earth. But that seems to be an entirely artificial reading of the text. Such a huge event would need to be described, but it is not even hinted at. Already we have noted that the seven churches in the previous two chapters could describe church life at any time in history, and that therefore those letters are always relevant. Chapters 4 – 18 describe events in heaven and on the earth before the return of Christ, which is then described in chapter 19. So we are reading of the church still on the earth, facing trials and tribulations, but also receiving assurance of the ultimate triumph and victory of Christ. This is a victory in which the church will share.

In the Spirit

We meet some difficult phrases, expressions and pictures in this chapter. For example, who are the four living creatures and the 24 elders? But some phrases are even more challenging than the technical or symbolic ones. There are words used that point to something far beyond our current experience, where John seems to be translated into a different realm altogether. John looks and sees a door standing open in heaven. How do we deal with that!? Of course, John is not the only one we read of in the Scriptures who had this kind of experience. Ezekiel tells us that he had visions of God, and, writing to the Corinthians, Paul speaks of being caught up to the third heaven. In Luke's account of the trial of Stephen, he records that the first Christian martyr rejoiced to see an open heaven and the glory of God (Acts 7:55–56).

With all the medical help available today to assist people, even in the moments of death, it may be that people's senses are dulled, which means that we do not hear so many wonderful deathbed stories as we once did. Billy Graham tells how, as he witnessed his grandmother's death, she opened her arms and said, "I see Jesus."

Clearly, there have been times when the door of heaven has been opened and people have glimpsed a dimension beyond this life.

Many commentators remark on the fact that this chapter reads as though John sees heaven open before he is in the Spirit (verses 1–2). We might expect it to have been the other way round, and perhaps it was, but it doesn't read like that. According to verse 1, John takes the initiative and looks. This could remind us of what Paul says in Colossians, "Since, then, you have been raised with Christ, set your hearts on things above, where Christ is seated at the right hand of God. Set your minds on things above, not on earthly things" (Colossians 3:1–2). We tend to think from an earthly perspective, immersed in the things of this world, but the Bible tells us to "think up" – to see ourselves seated in heavenly places!

Bertrand Russell, one of the great philosophers of the 20th century, once said, "When I die, I rot." Russell's philosophy is very dangerous. Philosophical ideas can get into the mainstream of a society's thinking, and can sow the seeds of a nation's destruction. Communism and Nazism each began as a philosophy and devastated whole nations. To say, "When I die, I rot", is as good as saying that we exist only by random chance, so that when we die we will be nothing, and our lives are without meaning. The outcome of that way of thinking is that there is no basis for an agreed morality, or for compassion. It's my life; I'll do with it, and with other people, just as I want. And why not? There's no purpose in us being here; we're only here as a freak accident.

In contrast to Russell's philosophy, John Calvin, considered by many to be the greatest theologian of all, once said, "I pity the man, I pity the woman who never thinks about heaven." We can all be great theologians. Think of things above, think of eternity, and contemplate heaven. John looked up and saw an open heaven. When we look up and see heaven and think about eternity, it makes all the difference to our lives here on earth. Of course, some suggest that we can be so heavenly minded that we are of no earthly use. But the reverse is usually true: the more heaven is in our view, the more we will contribute to this life. We realize that we are not here just for the present, but we live our lives in the light of that great day when we will be in heaven.

So we come to this other remarkable phrase, "I was in the Spirit." Perhaps what put John in the Spirit was that he was looking into heaven. You cannot easily be in the Spirit if your thinking is entirely secular and materialistic. Our experience of being in the Spirit may be limited because we tend to let earthly and worldly thinking dominate us. If we feel that we do not know about life in the Spirit, it is worth asking the question: What do we think about – what do we set our minds on? There is a dimension of life that can only be described as life in the Spirit, which seems to have been the daily experience of early believers as they constantly saw signs, wonders and many conversions. Modern, Western Christianity tends to be intellectual, and certainly we need clear content to our faith. But we mustn't let our faith be dominated by our intellect – we need to keep looking up, for that leads to life in the Spirit.

We need to be strong in the word of God, for that also leads to experiences of God. However, the word of God is not a substitute for experiences of God. Often we pray for the Spirit to come down, but we also need to look up.

In the world

We are told what John sees as he looks into this open heaven. What grabs his attention immediately is a throne with someone sitting on it. This is clearly the throne of God, mentioned at least fifteen times in chapters 4 and 5. A throne speaks of authority, and the one who sits on this heavenly throne wields absolute authority. What do we learn about this throne? What is it that catches our attention?

It is a place of radiance

The appearance of the one who sits on this throne is of jasper and carnelian. Though jasper could be any of several colours, the most valued type was green. Carnelian, on the other hand, is red. So the one who sits on the throne displays complementary colours of red and green, and this may be a pictorial way of indicating alpha and omega – the beginning and the end. A rainbow, "resembling an emerald", surrounds the throne. This is indeed a mystery, because the whole point about a rainbow is that it is not just one colour, but contains seven colours. But here there is a green rainbow and added to it is lightning, rumblings and peals of thunder (see Exodus 19:16 and Hebrews 12:18–19).

In chapter 1 we read of seven lamps and seven spirits of God, and these are described again here; this probably speaks of the fullness of the Holy Spirit. Before the throne there is a sea of glass, or rather what looks like a sea of glass. Many suggestions have been made about this, but the one that appeals to me most is that it speaks of God's absolute distance from man in sheer majestic holiness.

This is the radiance of God's throne. There is colour and sound and majesty and glory and holiness. John does his best to give us an adequate description of such an awesome sight.

It is a place of reigning

"Surrounding the throne were twenty-four other thrones, and seated on them were twenty-four elders. They were dressed in white and had crowns of gold on their heads" (verse 4). Although not every commentator agrees, it does seem most likely that these 24 elders represent the whole church of God; the number 24 is perhaps meant to speak of the twelve tribes of Israel, together with the twelve apostles of the Lamb (see verses 12 and 14 of Revelation 21). These then represent all the people of God, under the Old and New Covenants. This is the perspective of heaven. At whatever point we may be in history, and no matter what troubles she faces on the earth (and there will be plenty of them), the church is exalted to a place where she reigns. Paul, in Ephesians, speaks of believers being seated in heavenly realms, even while we are still on the earth. This gives us the confidence that on the earth, the church, even now, is able to function with the delegated authority of God. The kingdom steadily advances in the earth. The church should therefore look up and gain the perspective of heaven.

It is a place of reassurance

Wherever you look, and from wherever you look, we see that at every moment in history, God is on the throne. In some parts of the world it can be very tough for believers. Think of the situation for Christians in Saudi Arabia or southern Sudan; even where you live, it may seem very hard going. But look up! What do we see? God is on the throne.

It will certainly get tough in the future in the time of the great tribulation. There will be many martyrs who will come out of tribulation, but we read that Christians from that time will also be before the throne of God (7:15). Once again, this throne is central.

What is it that gains all our attention at the close of history? Again, it is the throne of God. "Then I saw a great white throne and him who was seated on it. Earth and sky fled from his presence, and there was no place for them" (20:11). This mention of the earth and the sky fleeing away surely indicates that on that day we will have eyes only for the throne of God.

We need to see the importance of this. The throne speaks of the God of history. In the time of the early church, John's readers would often have faced persecution. Many would have been slaves. Here was the reassurance they needed: God is still on the throne. Through the centuries of Christian history, when faithful believers have been opposed, persecuted and martyred, they too have needed the assurance that God is still on the throne. What gave a man like William Carey the courage to minister in pagan India, and to keep ministering for years before he saw his first convert? Or why would Whitfield risk his life repeatedly, crossing the Atlantic in small, frail boats, to preach the gospel in America? We could run through the names of thousands of men and women who have done mighty exploits for God, often in the face of great opposition or with seemingly small results. But all had the absolute confidence in the midst of their perils, suffering and even death, that God is still on the throne.

The church lives in the world throughout history. But at every point in history, and then at the end of history, a throne is established. It is a throne of radiant splendour, and the Lord Almighty sits on that throne. As the church, we should never forget this, whatever may come. Let us look up and be reassured, for although the church is in the world, God is on the throne.

In time

Around the throne, as well as 24 elders, there are four living creatures. They are covered with eyes; according to the commentators, this is difficult symbolism, but by reference to Ezekiel's vision of God, in which he saw eyes on the rims of wheels we may conclude that this speaks of God's total knowledge and understanding.

"The first living creature was like a lion, the second was like an ox, the third had a face like a man, the fourth was like a flying eagle" (verse 7). Several commentators suggest that these creatures are cherubim, representing the entire living creation. Four is the number of creation. Revelation itself speaks of the four corners and the four winds of the earth (7:1). The lion symbolizes all wild creatures, the ox all working and domestic animals, the flying eagle all birds. The fourth living creature represents mankind, created uniquely in God's image. All these creatures declare:

Holy, holy, holy
is the Lord God Almighty,
who was, and is, and is to come (verse 8)

Here there is worship of the Triune God by the whole of the living creation; the repetition of this cry, day after day, is a constant reminder of the eternal nature of God. He is the God of all history and it is good to be reminded that he acts in history, and that there is a day, in time, when he will come again. Paul speaks of God sending his Son in the fullness of time. There was a day when Christ was born, and a day when he was crucified. There was a day of Pentecost when the Holy Spirit was poured out. There will be a day in the future when Christ will come again, and this is the day known as the day of the Lord. We even date our calendar from the time of Christ's birth. God began history and he will finish it. God was, is, and is to come. Eventually, the last day in history will come. Jesus will return, and in so doing will fulfil over 300 Bible promises. That day will change everything for ever.

In us

The living creatures and the 24 elders continually bring praise to God in heaven:

> You are worthy, our Lord and God,
> to receive glory and honour and power,
> for you created all things,
> and by your will they were created
> and have their being (verse 11)

The last phrase of this song could literally be understood as, "because of your will they were created." The King James Version brings this out as, "for thy pleasure they are and were created." *The Message* reads, "it was created because you wanted it." The truth that comes through is that God created all things for his own pleasure.

The vastness of the universe is created for God's pleasure. All living creatures have been made for the pleasure of God. Self-centredness, though a vice in human beings, is actually a virtue in God. When people see themselves as the most important, it is a vice, for the simple reason that they are *not* the most important. But God actually *is* the most important, and therefore for him to regard himself in this way is entirely appropriate. He is the one who really is worthy of notice and service. And when God is our central focus, we will find our greatest joy. For his pleasure all things have been created. We worship God, we adore his majesty, but in so doing we ourselves find great joy and true satisfaction. This is what we are made for.

CHAPTER SIX

WORTHY IS THE LAMB
Revelation 5

Revelation chapters 4 and 5 very much stand together. The beginning of chapter 4, where John speaks of looking into an open heaven, really serves as an introduction to both chapters. John, who has been captivated by the throne of God, views the 24 elders and four living creatures. In this chapter John is still looking into an open heaven. What does he see?

The Angels

Here, and indeed in the whole of this book, we are made aware of a strong angelic presence in heaven. In verse 11, John reports seeing many angels. The Greek language is limited in its ability to express large numbers, but the sense conveyed is of myriads upon myriads of angels. Heaven is thick with angels. They are part of the vast assembly that worships God.

When we "join the church", as we often put it, we probably think of being joined to a group of people. But it's much more than that: we are also joined to multitudes of angels. "But you have come to Mount Zion, to the heavenly Jerusalem, the city of the living God. You have come to thousands upon thousands of angels in joyful assembly, to the church of the firstborn, whose names are written in heaven. You have come to God, the judge of

55

all men, to the spirits of righteous men made perfect" (Hebrews 12:22–23).

So when we come to Christ, we also come to a vast and varied company that is much bigger than we first realize. We may be tempted to look at our church or home group, and say, "Is this it?" Well, the answer is, "No, it isn't!" We are joined to so much more.

We come to the city of God, that is, to all the people of God, past, present and future. We come to God himself. We come to that part of the church now on earth but whose names are written in heaven. We come to all the saints who are already in heaven. We also come to those multitudes of angels in continual celebration. The company we join is really great in number and huge in variety.

Angels are free of problems and of sin. They don't get cross, sulk, ignore you, or do other upsetting things that people do. But they do make a lot of noise! "And I saw a mighty angel proclaiming in a loud voice . . ." (verse 2; see also 1 Thessalonians 4:16).

The reference to a mighty angel calls attention to the fact that angels are not clones. It is easy to think that they are all exactly alike; they are often represented like that in nativity scenes. But the fact that they are not flesh and blood does not mean that they are not individuals. John looks into an open heaven and sees a *mighty* angel.

Sometimes an angel is named, as Gabriel is. Gabriel seems to have prenatal insight and so is able to foretell a birth and the sex of the baby without a scan! Michael is named, as the archangel, and seems to be in a superior league to the rest of the angelic creatures.

John also sees four living creatures. These may represent all living creatures (see previous chapter), but they are also often identified with the cherubim of Ezekiel's prophecy. These cherubim belong to another, different order to that of the angels.

In Isaiah chapter 6 we read of the seraphim, who may be yet

another order of heavenly creatures. How exactly we should understand all these creatures may be beyond us; we just get the report of glimpses into an open heaven. It could certainly indicate that there might be at least as much variety in heaven as there is on the earth.

So we are joined, not just to a few people in a house group, or a few people in a local church, or even many more people at something like a national Bible Week celebration. We are also joined to seraphim, cherubim, archangels, mighty angels and multitudes of other angels.

The book of Hebrews tells us that angels serve those who inherit salvation. The full extent of that service to us we will only understand in eternity.

The scroll

John sees, in the right hand of God, a scroll sealed with seven seals. This is a very important feature of this chapter.

How are we to understand this scroll? Fortunately, though it is important, it is not difficult. Commentators broadly agree about this. The chapters that follow, telling us what happens when the seals are broken, give us the necessary clue. The scroll contains the judgements of God that will fall on the earth, but they conclude with the full establishment of God's government and rule. What has been written is complete. The scroll is written on both sides and sealed with seven seals. Another way of stating the significance of this scroll is to say that it contains God's plan, which is to be executed on the earth.

However, the scroll does more than contain information. The seals have to be broken; without this, the judgements of God cannot take place, and God's kingdom will not come. Breaking the seals does the job; it does not mean merely that the scroll is open and can now be read.

There is a very poignant question put by the mighty angel, in a loud voice, "Who is worthy to break the seals and open the scroll?" (verse 2). And, as John unfolds his vision to us, it seems at first that there is no answer to this question. Heaven, and, we sense, the entire universe, holds its breath. Is no one worthy to break the seals and open the scroll? John weeps and weeps. How else can God's work be done on the earth; how else can his kingdom come? Sometimes we can look at the world and wonder – will God's kingdom ever come? We too can feel like weeping.

But there is one who is worthy. "Then one of the elders said to me, 'Do not weep! See, the Lion of the tribe of Judah, the Root of David, has triumphed. He is able to open the scroll and its seven seals'" (verse 5).

This clearly is another description of Jesus Christ.

He is "the Lion of the tribe of Judah"

Here is one of many titles given to Jesus in Revelation. This particular one goes back to Genesis (49:9). We read there that the patriarch Jacob blessed his many sons. He said to Judah, "You are a lion's cub, O Judah." At one level this title reveals the truth that Jesus is one with us in human nature, for he is descended from the tribe and line of Judah. That household carried a promise that, through it, God would establish an everlasting kingdom (Genesis 49:10).

He is "the Root of David"

Jesus was descended from David according to the natural line of descent. However, in saying that Jesus is the *Root* of David, the point is made that he is also the eternal Son of God. In Revelation 22:16 Jesus is referred to as both "the Root and the Offspring of David". This corresponds to Jesus' own words, "before Abraham was born, I am!" (John 8:58)

He has triumphed

We know that the book of Revelation uses many symbols and pictures. At this point we might think that Jesus' triumph is incomplete until he has taken the scroll and broken the seals – that he has to do something else to complete his triumph. But this would be a mistake. Jesus, the God-Man, has already triumphed. His triumph has been achieved through his death and resurrection – symbolized in his taking the scroll and breaking the seals. The guarantee that the kingdom will come on the earth is Jesus' death and resurrection. What John is conveying is the absolute certainty of this. Because Jesus has triumphed, he has begun a chain of events that will bring in the kingdom in all its fullness.

The prophet Daniel said, "In my vision at night I looked, and there before me was one like a son of man, coming with the clouds of heaven. He approached the Ancient of Days and was led into his presence. He was given authority, glory and sovereign power; all peoples, nations and men of every language worshipped him. His dominion is an everlasting dominion that will not pass away, and his kingdom is one that will never be destroyed" (Daniel 7:13–14).

That is a glorious promise from the Old Testament; and here, in the book of Revelation, that promise is confirmed. He has triumphed. He takes the scroll and breaks the seals. I do not believe that the New Testament allows us to be triumphalistic, anticipating that the church will go from glory to glory with hardly a problem. The church is always going through some degree of tribulation, and there is the great tribulation to come. We can all too easily observe how much warfare and disaster there is in the world. Even at the level of our local church we are aware of weakness and backsliding. We too could easily weep and weep. But, "Do not weep! . . . the Lion of the tribe of Judah, the Root of David" – he *has triumphed.*

Disasters occurring throughout the centuries all signify that the seals are being opened, but finally God's kingdom will be established. "The earth will be filled with the knowledge of the glory of the Lord, as the waters cover the sea" (Habakkuk 2:14); all of history is most surely moving to that conclusion.

The Lamb

Having seen Jesus described as the Lion of Judah, we might expect to find a lion in the centre of the throne of God, but in fact what we see is a lamb (verse 6). But this is "a Lamb, looking as if it had been slain". In Revelation 1 we read of John falling as though dead before the Christ of glory. Here, John sees Christ again, but this time Christ is standing in the centre of the throne. So now we are being exposed to the Christ who forever bears the marks of sacrifice as an eternal reminder that he died for our sins, but who is standing, to emphasize that he also rose again.

At this point we must expand our normal understanding of a throne, as this one seems distinctly overcrowded with God seated and the Lamb standing! But the obvious symbolism conveys the sense of God's awesome majesty and lordship over history.

The Lamb has seven horns, representing strength and power. He has seven eyes with which he sees into all the earth. There is mention of the seven spirits, which speak of the fullness of the Spirit sent into all the earth. This all-powerful, all-seeing Christ who pours out the Holy Spirit is worthy to take the scroll. All heaven worships.

This passage helps us to resolve a dilemma. Is this Satan's earth, or God's earth?

The New Testament makes us fully aware of Satan's influence upon the earth. We can illustrate this with the verses: ". . . the whole world is under the control of the evil one" (1 John 5:19); "The god of this age has blinded the minds of unbelievers . . ." (2 Corinthians 4:4). In addition, John 14:30 refers to Satan as "the prince of this world".

This is the human perspective; this is how it often seems to be as we look at the state of the world. But as we read the book of Revelation, we are reminded that we need to look up. We can then view an authority which is above Satan. Jesus is the one who takes the scroll and breaks the seals. Around us we may feel that Satan is gaining victories and having his way upon the earth.

In fact, Jesus stands in the centre of the throne, and he rules over all things.

When the seventh seal is opened, the kingdom will come in all its fullness. The rule of God will be universally established, and Satan will be cast down for ever.

We can look at the world and get depressed. The remedy for this is to look up! The Lamb stands in the centre of the throne – a truth that should bring us to worship.

The blood

And they sang a new song:

"You are worthy to take the scroll and to open its seals,
because you were slain,
and with your blood you purchased men for God
from every tribe and language and people and nation.
You have made them to be a kingdom and priests to serve our
God,
and they will reign on the earth." (verses 9–10)

These verses talk of the power of the blood. They are so important in connection with evangelism and church planting. A guarantee is given here that men and women from every people group will be saved, and that guarantee is the blood of Jesus. The price has been paid in the blood of the Lamb, and it is amply sufficient to make such a vast and varied purchase.

In Matthew 24:14 Jesus says that every nation (or people group) would receive the gospel of the kingdom before the end of the age. In Revelation 7 we will read of those from every group of people worshipping before the throne of God. If Jesus has said it, if the blood of Christ has paid for it, if John has actually seen it, then it must be certain. There will be those in eternity from every people group who will worship Jesus.

This certainty makes all evangelism and church planting vital and worthwhile. This is what underwrites every missionary effort

– even to so-called "closed nations". There is no group from which Jesus will not have a people. There is no people group for whom Jesus' blood has not been shed for the purchase of a church. What has always motivated the greatest evangelists and missionaries is that there is no possibility of failure. We can say with absolute certainty that at some point there will be a response to the gospel from every people, because of the purchase of the blood of the Lamb.

People are not only purchased *by* God, but also *for* God (verse 9). It is actually for the pleasure of God that no people group will be left unrepresented by a church when the end comes. From every nation Christ will have his triumph: those who will enjoy God for ever and bring him pleasure, worship and praise.

There is a story that during the great Moravian missionary thrust, some Moravian believers gave themselves into slavery to share the gospel with those living in the most miserable of conditions. As they were taken away, they lifted their hands to heaven and cried, "May the Lamb receive the reward of his sufferings." These believers were confident that the purchase of blood would be effective even among the most wretched of people.

Verse 10 speaks in terms of God's kingdom. God's rule will be displayed through us. We will be priests offering worship, and we will reign on the earth. We do that a little now (Romans 5:17), but we will finally reign on a new earth as God's people, purchased by the power of the blood of the Lamb.

The worship

In chapters 4 and 5, the cry of "worthy" is recorded three times, and no wonder, for Christ has triumphed. He is the slain Lamb who stands in the centre of the throne. He has purchased people by his blood. He will oversee history and bring in the kingdom. He has taken the scroll and broken the seals.

The worship of Jesus is a complete worship. Seven aspects of adoration are described: "Worthy is the Lamb, who was slain, to receive power and wealth and wisdom and strength and honour and glory and praise!" (verse 12). The praise is universal in its scope, coming from myriads of angels, every creature, the four living creatures, and elders representing the whole church.

Today God is on the throne.

The seals are being opened.

God's kingdom will come.

And so:

WORTHY IS THE LAMB WHO WAS SLAIN!

CHAPTER SEVEN

THE SEVEN SEALS
Revelation 6

In Revelation 6, we read of six of the seven seals being opened.
We have to wait until chapter 8, verse 1 for the opening of the
seventh seal. These seven seals are:

Seal 1   The white horse
Seal 2   The red horse
Seal 3   The black horse
Seal 4   The pale horse
Seal 5   The cry of the martyrs
Seal 6   Cosmic shakings
Seal 7   Silence in heaven (8:1)

Like many commentators, I see the seven seals, seven trumpets
and seven bowls as all referring to the same historical events.
They each give a different perspective on the same matters.
Some see these as events occurring immediately before Christ's
return, whereas I see them as describing events that take place
across the entire span of Christian history.

It has often been noted that there are close parallels between
the eschatology of Mark 13 and that of Revelation 6. This can be
seen in the following lists:

Mark 13	Revelation 6
wars	wars
strife	strife
famine	famine
earthquakes	pestilence
persecution	persecution
cosmic shakings	cosmic shakings

At one level, the comparison of these two chapters illustrates the consistency of Scripture. But in Mark 13, is Jesus speaking just of the end of history, or is he giving an overview of all Christian history? Surely it is the latter. When Jesus speaks of wars and rumours of wars, he adds that "the end is still to come" (verse 7). Such conflicts have occurred and will occur throughout history. That is also true of persecution. Cosmic shakings, however, seem immediately to precede the end. In Revelation 6, we have the same kind of order. This therefore indicates that the chapter is describing the whole span of Christian history.

The first four seals form a group, since they describe the four horsemen of the Apocalypse. These seem to reflect what we read in Zechariah (6:1–3), where four groups of horses ride forth.

The white horse

"I watched as the Lamb opened the first of the seven seals" (verse 1). This is clearly a dramatic moment. "I looked and there before me was a white horse! Its rider held a bow, and he was given a crown, and he rode out as a conqueror bent on conquest" (verse 2).

We need to identify the rider of the horse. Some have suggested that it is Jesus, for in Revelation 19 Jesus rides on a white horse and wears many crowns. But this seems an odd interpretation, for, as it is Christ himself who breaks the seal, it would seem strange if he were then the rider. Also, this interpretation does not fit in with the next three riders, who are clearly bent on destruction and evil.

A better interpretation is that this represents a spirit of evil riding out into this world. Bent on conquest, it stirs up wars and rumours of wars. In the Old Testament a "bow" was a symbol of slaughter, and evil always rides out to kill. This rider was given a crown, and he represents those who seek power, and who want to crush and rule over others. It has always been like that – that is the condition of our world, and it will be like that until the end. The first world war was supposed to be the war to end all wars, but it was soon to be followed by the second world war. Only when Christ, the Prince of Peace, returns at the end will there be true peace established for ever.

The red horse

"Then another horse came out, a fiery red one. Its rider was given power to take peace from the earth and to make men slay each other. To him was given a large sword" (verse 4).

This clearly intensifies the conflict revealed by the first seal, and we see again a scene of strife. The reference to men slaying each other is seen by some as referring to civil war. Any war is terrible, but when those within a nation kill one another, the horror is greater still. Men who may have been at peace as neighbours for generations can suddenly turn to slaughter and atrocity. It happened when India and Pakistan were partitioned into separate nations in 1947: soldiers from these two countries, who had fought against a common enemy in the Burma campaign during the second world war, began to slaughter one another in their hundreds of thousands. It happened again at the end of the last century in the Balkans.

The end to such terrible atrocities will come finally, only when Jesus returns and his government is fully established.

The black horse

"I looked and there before me was a black horse! Its rider was holding a pair of scales in his hand. Then I heard what sounded like a voice among the four living creatures, saying, 'A quart of wheat for a day's wages, and three quarts of barley for a day's wages, and do not damage the oil and the wine!'" (verses 5–6).

There are different views on the meaning of this third seal. On one hand, it could point to a scarcity of basic foods, like wheat and barley, that therefore have to be measured carefully. It could refer to a time of famine when the prices are extortionate. On the other hand, is this describing luxury, with oil and wine as symbols of the good life? Certainly, worldwide, but often within the same nation, there are those who have little and are close to starvation, while at the same time there are others who have much and enjoy the "oil and the wine".

We have experienced the contrast ourselves as we watch pictures of starving children on the television while we pull the lid off a yoghurt pot. When will such famines and extreme inequalities come to an end? Only when Jesus returns to establish his kingdom and rule.

The pale horse

"I looked, and there before me was a pale horse! Its rider was named Death, and Hades was following close behind him. They were given power over a fourth of the earth to kill by sword, famine and plague, and by the wild beasts of the earth" (verse 8).

We have here a symbol of general pestilence upon the earth. This fourth seal probably sums up the previous three. Throughout history there has been death, war, famine and plague. In the Middle Ages, the terrifying Black Death killed over half the population of England, and the devastating AIDS epidemic of today is killing millions in Africa. Wild beasts tend to multiply where war has raged and where populations have been reduced. This fourth seal speaks of every type of pestilence upon the earth.

We read these serious descriptions in picture language, but they are our world's history. How do people cope without a hope in God? In our Western society it is easy enough to enjoy the "oil and the wine". We tend not to be touched by the mega-disasters known in other parts of the world. In our global village, we can live in comfort only a few hours' flying time away from terrible and obvious suffering. Yet even in our comfortable society there are many individuals around us with their own personal agonies and no hope.

We must live with an "until" in our spirit. For the world is like this: horsemen ride out to bring damage across the earth, *until* another will ride forth on a white horse. There will be crowns on his head and a proclamation: King of kings and Lord of lords!

As these first four seals are opened, and just before each horseman rides forth, one of the living creatures shouts, "Come!" This "Come!" could be read simply as a call to each rider, but I think that it is something else.

In Revelation 4 and 5, the four living creatures represent the whole created order. At present, creation is in bondage to decay, awaiting its day of deliverance and freedom. Redeemed men and women everywhere are conscious of the world's sufferings and see the desperate need for God's rule to break in. What is the longing of creation? What is the longing in our spirits? Surely something expressed only in the cry of "Come!" As they look at the agonies of the world, the four living creatures say, "Come!" It is surely a cry to Jesus to come and put the whole thing right.

God, help us not to be so lulled by the oil and wine that there fails to be a "Come!" in our spirit.

The cry of the martyrs

"When he opened the fifth seal, I saw under the altar the souls of those who had been slain because of the word of God and the testimony they had maintained. They called out in a loud voice, 'How long, Sovereign Lord, holy and true, until you judge the inhabitants of the earth and avenge our blood?' Then each of them was given a white robe, and they were told to wait a little longer, until the number of their fellow-servants and brothers who were to be killed as they had been was completed" (verses 9–11).

This too describes a situation that occurs right across church history. In every century there have been martyrs for the faith. "The outcry is symbolic of the necessity of ultimate justice, of the final righteousness of God which is to be revealed . . . it is an outcry that ascends to the throne of God throughout all the history of the church in the world" (Herman Hoeksema, *Behold He Cometh*, p. 226). This should not be seen as a cry for revenge, but rather, for justice.

What we read of as taking place when this seal is opened is exactly in line with the teaching of Jesus on persecution. Why is it that the souls are under the altar? In Jewish thought, this was a place of honour.

These verses suggest that there is a specific number who are to be martyred before the end of history, just as Revelation 7 suggests that specific number who are to be saved. These numbers are vast beyond our ability to count, and therefore unknown. Neither number has yet been reached. More will yet be saved, and more will yet be martyred. Sometimes the story of a martyrdom reaches the headlines, but often we will not even hear of them.

The martyrs cry out, asking how long it will be before God demonstrates his justice. The response to their cry is that they must wait a little longer. There is a tension here. John can speak in his first letter of it being the last hour. But we are now 2,000 years further on in Christian history! How do we reconcile the promise that Christ's coming will be soon with all the centuries that have gone by since the promise was made? Of course, this raises difficult questions about the nature of time that is controlled by a God who is himself eternal. But the Bible always points to an absolute and certain end. A man of 95 knows that he must be very near the end of his life. A young teenager hears that life is "soon over" and smiles. But the years roll on, and eventually all of us will be gone. Even to the teenager, the "soon" points to a certain end.

The martyrs will be avenged. Just a little while longer, and suddenly the end will come. It is certain.

Cosmic shakings

The end of Revelation 6 reads very like the end of Mark 13. "At that time men will see the Son of Man coming in clouds with great power and glory" (Mark 13:26).

The shaking of everything in the cosmos will tell us that we are finally at the end. At that time, look up, for Christ is about to appear.

Revelation obviously uses symbolic language here; we read of every mountain being removed, but then of people hiding among the mountains. At the end, everything is shaken, but the followers of the Lamb will know that their redemption is near. At this point in the book, we are brought to the very brink of Christ's return, but then in the next chapter John breaks away to another subject. It is not until chapter 19 that Christ's return is described. But once the sixth seal has been opened, we do stand at the end of history.

Hebrews 12 also reminds us that there will be a shaking of all things, which will undermine all that this world is building for. Even on a small scale, we can be zealous to build a comfortable life, although we are vulnerable to storm, fire, flood or earthquake. On a larger scale, people build as though this life is everything, when actually it will all be shaken to pieces one day.

There is nothing in *this* world in which to place our ultimate confidence. But Hebrews 12:28–29 gives us great encouragement: "Therefore, since we are receiving a kingdom that cannot be shaken, let us be thankful, and so worship God acceptably with reverence and awe, for our God is a consuming fire."

In this world the horsemen ride out. On the large scale, there is war and famine and pestilence and martyrdom. Is life pointless? Is it just a sick joke? Will it get worse and worse until we end up destroying ourselves? No! Creation groans, but will be redeemed when Jesus comes again. Martyrs cry out, "How long?", but will be vindicated when Jesus returns. Everything will be shaken to pieces, but this world will give way to a new heaven and earth "that cannot be shaken". And that is the kingdom that we belong to.

The cry to Jesus is, "Come!" However, the seals must be opened before the Son of God appears to clear up the mess.

But we can be certain that he is coming soon.

CHAPTER EIGHT

THE SECURITY OF THE CHURCH
Revelation 7

Revelation chapter 7 presents an interlude between the opening of the sixth and seventh seals. It describes the safety of the people of God. The opening of the six seals in the previous chapter, and all the disasters that fall on the earth, could raise the question, "Who can survive all of this?" The seventh chapter of Revelation gives its answer by showing us the security of believers.

A seal

At the beginning of the chapter, John sees four angels holding back four winds from blowing on the earth. This may be another way of describing the four horsemen of chapter 6, and, because they are held back, it introduces the theme of security for the people of God.

Before these disasters fall on the earth, John sees another angel coming from the east, holding the seal of the living God. In the Bible, blessing often comes from the east. Paradise was in the east (Genesis 2:8); glory came to the temple from the east (Ezekiel 43:2); the star of Bethlehem was seen in the east (Matthew 2:2).

The seal that the angel brings is placed on the foreheads of

144,000 people. Who are these 144,000? I believe that it would be a superficial interpretation to see them either as Jews or Jewish believers, even though the number 144,000 is made up from "all the tribes of Israel" (verses. 4–8). The New Testament deals in detail with the nation of Israel, and specifically talks of Israel turning to Jesus as the Messiah before the end (Romans chapters 9–11). However, this is not the issue in the book of Revelation. The figure 144,000, made up of 12,000 drawn from each tribe, is very clearly a symbol, not a statistic. The listing of the tribes is not even the one that would have been most obvious in John's day. There is a feeling here of completeness: 12,000 from twelve tribes. It is reasonable to see this as a symbol of all the people of God – believing Jews and believing Gentiles.

There are a number of factors that seem to confirm this. In verse 3 the seal is put on the servants of God; in other words, on all believers. If one tries to be literal by saying that this number must be made up only of Jews, then one has to remain literal and say that there are exactly 12,000 true believers from each tribe, which is clearly highly unlikely.

In chapter 14 we meet the 144,000 again. There they are referred to as those redeemed from the earth (verse 3) and those who follow the Lamb (verse 4). Again, this indicates all the people of God.

Also, in chapters 13 and 14 we read that everyone who does not belong to God is given another type of seal, the mark of the Beast. Every person therefore receives a seal, either from God or from the Beast. There are no people without some seal. This indicates yet again that the 144,000 symbolize all of God's people. They receive the seal of God and so are preserved and kept safe.

The word "seal" is used in several different ways. A seal can be used as a prevention against harm, which is why an electric meter is sealed. A seal can represent a mark of ownership, which is why cattle are branded or sealed. It can represent authenticity, as when Paul told the church at Corinth that they were the seal of his apostleship (1 Corinthians 9:2). When the people of God are sealed, we can understand it to mean preservation from harm and the fact that we belong to God as his authentic children.

Despite the winds, horsemen and disasters that are to come, believers are sealed and will be kept safe. Destruction may fall on the earth, but the church is indestructible.

Salvation

What John sees next is a great multitude standing before the throne of God (verse 9). What is this great multitude? Again, the answer is surely that it is made up of the complete number of the people of God. Before, they were represented symbolically by the number 144,000; the actual number is too great for anybody to count.

Here we are seeing the people of God from two points of view. From the beginning of history they are sealed, so that throughout all disasters on the earth they *will* be kept safe. At the end of history, we see that they *have* been kept safe, and the total number stand in front of the throne of the Lamb.

This calls our attention to some important points about salvation.

A vast number will be saved

It is unfortunate that reformed Christianity is often represented as teaching the salvation of small numbers. The number of God's elect, whom God has sealed and will keep safe, is vast. It is so vast that the Bible has to use the symbol of 144,000, or to state that the number is too big to count. The number to be saved is likened elsewhere to the stars in the sky or the sand on the shore. There is an actual number, but it is "beyond counting". We can be confident that in our own nation, many more will yet be saved and added to the church before Christ returns.

Prophecy is fulfilled

Jesus said, "And this gospel of the kingdom will be preached in the whole world as a testimony to all nations, and then the end will come" (Matthew 24:14). At the end of history, there will be some from every nation, or people group, who will for eternity be worshippers of God. What John saw was the fulfilment of Jesus' promise, "a great multitude that no-one could count, from every nation, tribe, people and language, standing before the throne and in front of the Lamb" (Revelation 7:9).

The gospel will be preached to all peoples, and as long as this world remains, we must assume there are still some people groups to be reached. But to every one of these God's salvation will surely come.

Salvation results in joy

The redeemed in front of the throne hold palm branches, speaking of victory and joy. They give their praise in a loud voice and all heaven joins in:

> Amen!
> Praise and glory
> and wisdom and thanks and honour
> and power and strength
> be to our God for ever and ever.
> Amen! (verse 12)

Our salvation should always result in joyful praise. Even now we can experience a joy which Peter in his first letter describes as "inexpressible and glorious" (1 Peter 1:8). Before the throne of God we will experience the thrill and wonder of salvation with eternal joy.

We are going to be so happy. In fact, the major difference between now and then is that we will be happier. But we will not be more secure than now, for we are already sealed for the day of salvation. There may be storms, disasters and tragedies, but we are secure. Nothing can separate us from the love of God. The living God marks his people. They are sealed. They have a preservation order on them. Even in eternity you cannot be more secure than now. But you *will* be more happy.

> More happy, but no more secure
> The glorified saints now in heaven.

In heaven nothing will diminish our joy, or mar our happiness.

Salvation is from God

"Salvation belongs to our God" (verse10). It is the sovereign God who saves us. All our confidence is placed in him. The God who started it will finish it. This is our confidence: salvation belongs to the Lord.

The longer I am a Christian, the more convinced I become that if my salvation depended at all on me, I would have blown it a million times. It is God who gives salvation, who seals and who preserves. Before time, he predestined us. In time, he called us. Right now, he has justified us. In the future, he will glorify us. We simply receive what God gives. That really is good news! In glory we might want to ask someone else before the throne, "How did *you* get in?" The answer will always be: "Salvation belongs to our God." That's how they all got in. And that is how we will all get in.

Shelter

John says that one of the elders (in heaven) asks him a question. "These in white robes – who are they, and where did they come from?" (verse 13)

John answers, "Sir, you know." Then the elder says, "These are they who have come out of the great tribulation; they have washed their robes and made them white in the blood of the Lamb" (verse 14).

Obviously, to speak of robes washed *white* in *blood* is symbolism that strongly states the effectiveness of Christ's death for the complete cleansing of sinful people. Here we also see that the redeemed have come out of "great tribulation". This chapter indicates that they were sealed before the tribulation, and stand before the throne of God after they have come out of tribulation.

The details of the great tribulation will occupy us later, but it would be a mistake to see tribulation as something that the church will only have to endure right at the end. It would be an even bigger mistake to take the view that the church is removed before the tribulation. There is no scripture that clearly teaches that, and Revelation certainly doesn't. We can see that at the end of history trouble will intensify for the church. We will see later that there is a specific Antichrist who will arise in world history, but John's first letter also speaks of "many antichrists," which are already in the world (1 John 2:18–20).

One of our dangers as Christians is that we can judge events in the present and future from our present standpoint. Western Christians still suffer no real persecution and so we can easily think of the tribulation as something to come in the future – and some even hope to be raptured before it happens! But Western Christianity at the beginning of the 21st century is not typical of all church life. In history, and even now around the world in countries like China, Sudan and India, the church is already passing through great tribulation. The church always gets to glory out of tribulation. However, we will see that Revelation does teach about a more intense and universal trouble – the great tribulation – yet to come.

The church comes out of trouble into shelter. We see here the redeemed before the throne of God. They serve in the temple (verse 15); there is no temple in heaven except for God himself, so this must mean that they live forever in his presence and therefore under his protection.

The troubles of this world will no longer be troubles, whether hunger, or scorching heat, or sadness; whether they are the results of "natural" disasters, of sin, or of persecution.

When you think of heaven, do you think of it as a place where you will have no needs or desires? Doesn't that seem rather flat, dull and passive? Would it be a life of any interest at all? Surely, we *will* have needs and desires, but every one will be fully satisfied. We will have a Shepherd to lead us to springs of living water. Such shelter is promised to the people of God.

So far, we have not answered a huge question – what about now? We can talk of safety, but what about now? Does God keep us safe now? What about Luke 21:18, where we are promised that not a hair of our head shall perish? Plenty of Christians seem to be living in denial of this scripture!

In trying to answer this question, we need to say firstly that God works *continuously*. Let's consider two translations of Romans 8:28. In the King James Version it reads, "And we know that all things work together for good to them that love God, to them who are called according to his purpose." The New International Version is slightly different: "And we know that in all things God works for the good of those who love him, who have been called according to his purpose.'

Although both translations are possible, I suggest that the NIV is right here. In the present, Christians are not immune from "all things". They can know accident, disease, disability, unemployment and other misfortunes. But "all things" also includes good things, such as marriage, promotion and an inheritance. It is not that "all bad things work together for good." Actually, some bad things seem to help Christians to mature, and good things sometimes seem to ruin them.

I do not believe (as the King James Version suggests) that all things work together for my good. Over 30 years of pastoral experience tell me that not all things work for the good of all the members of my church. But surely the NIV is right when it tells us that God works for our good in all things. God is able to bring good things out of the greatest disasters and out of the most wonderful blessings – in fact, out of "all things". God works continuously.

Secondly, God also works *mysteriously*. C. H. Spurgeon once told the story of a widower who took his young children to look at a new house. The children disappeared into the cellar, quickly to return with the extraordinary claim that they had seen their mother. The father went to investigate, only to discover a deep well at the bottom of the cellar stairs. The children had been saved from falling into it by the "vision" they had seen.

In Acts 12 we read that in one particular persecution, James was martyred, but Peter was delivered from prison. God works mysteriously. Christianity is no guarantee of a trouble-free life. Yet sometimes God does intervene extraordinarily, and gives amazing deliverances.

Thirdly, God works *eternally*. It seems to me that the Christian church is inevitably heading for major conflict with worldly powers. Abortion is legal, we are told that homosexual relationships are valid, and euthanasia is increasingly considered as a valid option. These are all signs of the outworking of a philosophy that tells us that we are evolved creatures existing by mere chance. But we, as Christians, have a different viewpoint: God created the universe, he created us, and at death we face God, judgement and eternity. We live in the light of that view, and therefore our guarantee is one of eternal safety.

The horsemen ride forth. The church will always come to glory out of tribulation. But we will for ever be sheltered and satisfied by the Shepherd of our souls. We will be eternally safe and eternally secure.

CHAPTER NINE

THE SEVEN TRUMPETS
Revelation 8 and 9

As we come to these chapters, it is worth comparing the list of the seven trumpets with the list of the seven seals. Both describe judgements that fall upon the earth up to the close of history and the ushering in of the fullness of God's kingdom.

The seven seals	The seven trumpets
1. A white horse	1. Disasters on the land
2. A red horse	2. Disasters at sea
3. A black horse	3. Disasters on rivers
4. A pale horse	4. Disasters in the heavens
5. The cry of the martyrs	5. Attacks on minds and emotions
6. Cosmic shakings	6. Disasters of every kind
Interlude: the security of the church	Interlude: the ministry and mission of the church
7. Silence in heaven	7. Noise in heaven

The prayers of the saints

The passage begins with seven angels who stand before God and are given seven trumpets. The trumpet is used many times in Scripture and in various ways – to give a warning, to

81

announce a victory, to gather the people and to awaken the dead.

However, before we read of the trumpets being blown, there is a reference to the prayers of all the saints. These are added to the incense that rises to God. When these prayers are presented to God they provoke a startling response: "Then the angel took the censer, filled it with fire from the altar, and hurled it on the earth; and there came peals of thunder, rumblings, flashes of lightning and an earthquake" (verse 5).

If the seven seals and seven trumpets give us an insight into the type of events taking place throughout the history of the church, this verse probably refers to the prayers of all the saints, right up to the end of the age.

We need to bear in mind that Revelation is a book about the victory of God. We will read of the return of Christ, the coming of the kingdom and the new heaven and new earth. For this reason, in Revelation 4 and 5 the exhortation has been to look up, for God is on the throne. The church may be under pressure, but every believer is marked with the seal of God and so nothing can finally harm her.

But what is the church doing throughout history? The prayers of all the saints are rising like incense, with the result described in verse 5 (quoted above). In our prayers we often ask for God's intervention. Certainly, we also give him our praise and worship, but we keep asking God to come. The Lord's Prayer says: "Let your kingdom come"; this is a cry for God to intervene upon the earth. And that kingdom will come, but not without judgements, thunder, rumblings, lightning, and earthquakes. There is of course a tension here. God is sovereign; he knows, he acts; and yet he requires us to pray to perfect his sovereign will. Prayer is not just a spiritual discipline with no clear outcome, so that it makes no difference whether we pray or not. Our prayers have real effect.

I would even suggest that prayer can be effective in changing God's mind! In Jonah (3:4) we read that the word of God was, "Forty more days and Nineveh will be overturned." The Ninevites believed this word of the Lord and turned to God with prayer and fasting, with the express purpose of changing God's mind; and he did change it. "When God saw what they did and how they turned from their evil ways, he had compassion and did not bring upon them the destruction he had threatened" (Jonah 3:10).

It is important to recognize that God does not change his mind in a fickle way, but only within the parameters of his own right-eousness. If we live in sin, the wrath of God will fall on us; but if we repent and pray, God changes his mind and brings us salvation.

So our prayers *are* effective. We are praying that God will intervene. There is a cumulative effect of all the prayers of all the saints, and this will play its part in bringing in the kingdom, through a process of judgements that will fall on the earth, leading up to the return of the King.

Natural disasters

The first four trumpets of chapter 8 cover what are usually referred to as natural disasters. They approximate to the four horsemen who ride out and cause troubles on the earth as the four seals are broken. These disasters seem to reflect the plagues of Egypt in Moses' time, but here they are depicted on a cosmic scale. There is hail, polluted water, darkness and, in chapter 9, locusts.

The first trumpet is blown, and hail and fire fall on the earth with devastating effects on the land, the trees and the grass. Some have suggested that this could be the result of nuclear fall-out, but that would narrow this event into a very small (if indeed any) part of history. We should rather see this as dealing with the whole sweep of history. A succession of disasters come to the earth – we can think of volcanoes, as well as other crises that affect the land, the trees and the grass. Some fifteen years before the book of Revelation was written, Mount Vesuvius erupted and buried the cities of Pompeii and Herculaneum in a hail of dust and stones. Such disasters have always been part of history, and will be to the end.

The second trumpet is blown, and disasters occur at sea. A third of the sea is turned to blood. We have certainly seen the sea covered in oil in tanker disasters in recent decades. With them comes the destruction of fish stocks and sea life. And there have been plenty of disasters at sea; the sinking of the *Titanic* is notorious, but ships are wrecked in storms and accidents almost every day, with consequent adverse effects on commerce and trade.

The third trumpet is blown, and a star called Wormwood falls from the sky and pollutes the rivers and streams. This is obviously symbolic, because there is a plant called wormwood that is bitter and poisonous. Over the years, we have increasingly seen the pollution of fresh water. Today, the most urgent need in the third world is very often for fresh, unpolluted drinking water.

The fourth trumpet is blown, and there is trouble in the heavens and partial darkness. There is some uncertainty about the correct interpretation here. In what sense in history has there been disaster in the heavens? Surely an eclipse, which might be read into this, is not a disaster. Could this be a reference to changes in the climate that will seriously affect the earth? What is certain is that at the end of history the heavens will be shaken, and there will be terrors upon the earth. However, that will be the time for believers to look up, for their redemption is at hand. Maybe we should understand this darkness as fundamentally spiritual, since it affects so many.

I have been to parts of Africa where there is gross spiritual darkness accompanied by great fear. People live in terror of ancestral spirits, offence against whom is believed to bring real troubles. There are farmers whose success leads to people burning down their houses on the grounds that they must have been using witchcraft. The result is that most people are frightened even to try to succeed.

These natural disasters affect the lives of many, but certainly not all, so repeatedly we read of "a third": a third of the trees are burned, a third of the ships are destroyed and a third of the rivers are polluted. Similarly, a third of the day is without light. Numbers in Revelation are often symbolic and not literal. But what does this number mean? It could refer to the fact that those judgements that fall on the earth in history are partial and not total. We all accept that natural disasters often occur at a level that affects many people. A third is only a part of the whole, but it is a significant part.

There are enough disasters to challenge men's security and make them think about their lives. To many of us in the West, earthquakes can seem remote, particularly when they occur in areas with little population. We can almost dismiss these events. But sometimes they come with devastating results to towns and cities. Similarly, we may hear of a fishing boat going down every five years or so with several people on board – we are sorry, but it hardly affects us. Sometimes, however, it is the *Titanic* that sinks, or a crowded ferryboat in the East, or even a cross-Channel ferry out of Dover. Without warning, the twin towers of the World Trade Centre are destroyed by terrorists. Then, suddenly, we are insecure and think, "It could have been me." Sometimes we know people caught up in these big disasters. There are certainly enough disasters, natural and man-made, to cause people to think: Do I need God? Should I get right with God? But do they?

Torments

"Torments" is a dramatic word, but one which seems to do justice to the fifth and sixth trumpets of Revelation 9. However, immediately before we read of the blowing of these trumpets, John says, "As I watched, I heard an eagle that was flying in mid-air call out in a loud voice: 'Woe! Woe! Woe to the inhabitants of the earth, because of the trumpet blasts about to be sounded by the other three angels!'" (8:13). These three woes are about to be revealed in the blowing of the last three trumpets. The first four trumpets sounded bad enough, with their range of natural disasters. But the next three trumpets speak of events that touch many people even more directly, and are therefore referred to as "woes".

There is a huge amount of symbolism involved with the fifth and sixth trumpets, which draws heavily on the Old Testament and other ancient Jewish literature. What we see, in common with other apocalyptic literature, is like an impressionist painting rather than photographic detail, and this needs to be borne in mind in any attempt to interpret these verses.

When the fifth trumpet is blown, locusts with stings like scorpions are released from "the Abyss". These attack people, though not those with "the seal of God upon their foreheads". There are certainly some vivid impressions conveyed here.

"During those days men will seek death, but will not find it; they will long to die, but death will elude them" (9:6). This could refer to a tormenting of people's minds and emotions, brought on, for example, by philosophies of despair. Individuals can be tormented in their minds, sink into acute depression and feel no hope. Life seems not worth living, and they have no faith in God to give any hope for when they die. Certainly, vast numbers of people suffer such torments even at the present time. We also read in verse 11 of Abaddon and Apollyon, which both mean "destroyer". They could be read as names of Satan's power. This could give us a key to understanding the locusts, which may represent demonic forces ruled over by Satan and causing great suffering in the world, so much so that sometimes individuals despair of life itself.

The sixth trumpet announces the second woe. Angels who have been bound at the river Euphrates are released, and so many millions of troops ride forth to bring plague, injury and death upon the earth. The mention of the Euphrates is significant because so much disaster had already come to the world from that region. In the Old Testament, the Assyrians and Babylonians had come from there. At the time that John was writing, the Euphrates marked the eastern boundary of the Roman empire, and beyond that lay the threat of the barbarians. The Euphrates therefore represents a source of danger.

In verse 18 we read, "A third of mankind was killed by the three plagues of fire, smoke and sulphur that came out of their mouths." But what does all this mean? It could refer to all the disasters that fall on the human race directly by plague, war and death. From human history we could give thousands of examples. At the beginning of the 21st century the AIDS epidemic sweeping across southern Africa is of plague proportions. Almost every day, the television shows conflict from somewhere in the world. Yesterday it was in the Balkans, today it might be in Israel, and tomorrow it could be anywhere.

Again, the judgement is partial. One third of humanity is killed. As we saw above, this is a symbolic but significant figure. Terrible events will challenge our security and make us think about our lives. Don't we need God?

So what shall we do?

Throughout history the church is praying. These prayers, which God always hears, play a real part in bringing in the kingdom, which will most surely come. There is a seventh seal and there is a seventh trumpet. But we live before the final victory of God in a world that suffers judgements. These judgements are not yet total, but surely they are severe enough to cause people to consider how they stand before God.

Yet we read, "The rest of mankind that were not killed by these plagues still did not repent of the work of their hands; they did not stop worshipping demons, and idols of gold, silver, bronze, stone and wood – idols that cannot see or hear or walk. Nor did they repent of their murders, their magic arts, their sexual immorality or their thefts" (9:20–21). What a story! No matter how loudly God shouts in judgement, people stop their ears and go on with their idols and sin and new age religions and immorality. So many live only for their money and possessions, which will be quite useless at death. It is, tragically, an old, old story. Think of the pharaoh in Moses' time, whose heart was hardened in the face of continuing judgements.

M. Wilcock comments,

The death-dealing horsemen of the sixth trumpet are not tanks and planes; or not only tanks and planes. They are also cancers and road accidents and malnutrition and terrorist bombs and peaceful demises in nursing homes. Yet "the rest of mankind, who were not killed by these plagues", still do not repent of their idolatry, the centering of their lives on anything rather than God, or of the evils which inevitably flow from it. They hear of pollution, of inflation, of dwindling resources, of blind politicians, and will not admit that the first four trumpets of God are sounding. In the end they themselves are affected by these troubles, and for one reason or another life becomes a torment: the locusts are out, Trumpet 5 is sounding, but they will not repent. Not even when the angels of the Euphrates rise to the summons of Trumpet 6, and the cavalry rides out to slay – by any kind of destruction, not necessarily war – a friend or a relative, a husband or a wife: not even in bereavement will they repent. "God whispers to us in our pleasures, speaks in our conscience, but shouts in our pains" (C. S. Lewis). If we will not hear the tremendous voice of the pains of bereavement, there can be no hope for us. (M. Wilcock, *The Message of Revelation*, IVP, 1975, p. 99)

These two chapters can be read either as full of doom and gloom, or full of grace. Surely, what these judgements are saying is, "Listen, get right with God." They are actually an offer of grace. They shout a warning, they call for repentance, but they offer grace. "Do you show contempt for the riches of his kindness, tolerance and patience, not realizing that God's kindness leads you towards repentance?" (Romans 2:4). Until the return of Jesus, the offer of his grace remains open to all.

CHAPTER TEN

THE CHURCH IN CONFLICT
Revelation 10 and 11

Between the opening of the sixth and seventh seals there was an interlude which described the security of the church amidst the judgements that fall upon the earth. Between the blowing of the sixth and seventh trumpets there is a similar interlude; this describes the ministry and mission of the church during times of conflict.

The mysteries of God

In the book of Revelation we not only read of angels but of mighty angels. Some have suggested that the mighty angel here (10:1) is actually Christ. He is described as "coming down from heaven", "robed in a cloud, with a rainbow above his head", and with a face "like the sun". But Jesus is more than an angel, however mighty, although this particular angel surely reflects the glory of Christ.

He holds a scroll (to which we will return) and plants one foot on the sea and one foot on the land. This speaks of God's authority over the whole earth. A conquest is often represented in Scripture by the placing of opposition under the victor's feet.

Revelation keeps telling us about God's victory. This is necessary, for in this world we can wonder: Is God really in control?

Chapters 4 and 5 have already helped us to look up and see God on the throne, sovereign over all history. Now, this vision of God's angel, with his feet planted on the land and the sea, shows us that he is also sovereign over the whole world.

It is important to recognize that the book of Revelation is about the triumph of God. Before that is described in detail, we see the events of history in woes, troubles and judgements. But through all of this there is a process taking place which will finally culminate in God's total victory.

At this point, halfway through a book, we could be tempted to take a look at the end to see how it all works out. Read chapters 21 and 22 and you will see that God wins!

The mighty angel shouts with the roar of a lion. Angels can be noisy. Some people who like quiet church services may find heaven rather a surprise! This angel's shout starts a chain reaction: the "voices of . . . seven thunders" speak, and John is about to write down what they say, when rather mysteriously we read, "I heard a voice from heaven say, 'Seal up what the seven thunders have said and do not write it down'" (10:4).

These seven thunders seem to reflect Psalm 29, where the voice of the Lord is said to thunder out seven times. Likewise, here in Revelation, the voice of the Lord thunders out. What does he say? John is not allowed to write it down, so we don't know, although there has been plenty of wild guessing!

Perhaps we are being reminded here that there are things in God that are mysteries, even for the church. We don't know it all: sometimes there are matters that are sealed up, and that we cannot understand. 1 Corinthians 13:12 talks about us looking through a glass dimly ("squinting in a fog, peering through a mist", as *The Message* puts it). But there will come a time in the future when we will see God face to face, and all will then become clear.

There is mystery enough in the Trinity: one God in three Persons. There is further mystery concerning Christ on the cross: we read both that "God was reconciling the world to himself in Christ" (2 Corinthians 5:19) and that Jesus cried out to the Father that he was utterly forsaken. Yet again, Jesus will return and "every eye will see him", and that on a round planet – so there are mysterious elements in that too.

But though there are many mysteries in God, what we do know clearly is that there is one God, that Christ died for our sin, and that Jesus will come again. So we have light, we have revelation, but we also live with mysteries; for now, some things are sealed up.

Some of the things that we do know now are incredible. But there are things that we do not know now which may well be even more incredible. Certainly, God is more amazing than we can possibly ever know. Who has been God's counsellor? Who has given God advice? Who can trace out God's works? Often, like Paul, we can only stand in amazement at the wonders of God, and this will naturally lead us to worship.

John seals up what the seven thunders say. There is a reminder here to remain humble in the face of mystery and to retain a sense of wonder. One day, there will be a full revelation. "But in the days when the seventh angel is about to sound his trumpet, the mystery of God will be accomplished" (10:7). All that has been sealed up will be revealed. We realize that in these days there is a huge amount of information available on the Internet. But that is nothing compared to what we shall know one day.

The angel announces that there will be no more delay – we are moving towards the seventh and final trumpet.

The word of God

The mighty angel holds a little scroll, and the word "little" is not unimportant. This is not a large document, but it is significant because it contains the word of God. There is speculation about what exactly is written there. Is it some of the scriptures from Revelation? If so, then what part of the book is written down? There are clearly parallels here with the scroll of Revelation 5. This word must be proclaimed, and so, at the end of chapter 10, John is told to prophesy again.

John now takes the scroll and eats it; it then becomes sweet in his mouth but sour in his stomach. This says three things to the church about the word of God.

We need to digest it – we do not live by physical bread alone. Our life is based on the truth that proceeds from God. This is our food, and it nourishes us in the Christian life. On one occasion, I had to leave an African country with some Christian friends who were being thrown out, on a visa technicality, from the church planting work they were doing there. I will always remember how, on a hazardous journey south, the wife of this couple constantly recalled and repeated passages from Scripture, which fed our souls at an anxious time.

We should enjoy it – for John this scroll was sweet like honey in the mouth. That speaks of enjoying the word of God.

We must proclaim it – this is where the word of God can become sour, for some people will reject it, abuse us because we deliver it, and scorn the truth. For our part, we need to keep enjoying the honey.

The church of God

The central plot of these two chapters (10 and 11) concerns the church in conflict.

John is told to measure the temple of God and count the worshippers (11:1). This is not a sudden reference to the temple in Jerusalem, which anyway had probably been destroyed about 25 years earlier by the Romans. But in harmony with the rest of the New Testament, the word "temple" becomes an expression for the church; it is the place where God lives in a fuller way: "For we are the temple of the living God" (2 Corinthians 6:16). Speaking of the people of God, Paul says, "In him the whole building is joined together and rises to become a holy temple in the Lord" (Ephesians 2:21). Again, "you also, like living stones, are being built into a spiritual house to be a holy priesthood, offering spiritual sacrifices acceptable to God through Jesus Christ" (1 Peter 2:5).

So we, the people of God, are God's house or temple. By telling John to measure and to count, God is again emphasizing our security. He knows us. He already knows the measurements and the numbers. This recalls the interlude between the sixth and seventh seals when the church of God is sealed. The church belongs to God; she is eternally secure. By contrast, in the outer courts of the temple are the unbelievers, who are not measured. This reflects the fact that when there was an actual stone temple in Jerusalem, Gentiles (those outside the people of God) were only allowed to enter the outer courts.

John now briefly introduces the subject of tribulation, which he will speak of more fully in chapter 13. John seems to be suggesting that the church is always going through a degree of tribulation. She knows pressure, persecution and difficulty. This happens throughout history, although its severity varies from time to time and from place to place. Towards the very end of history, the church will endure the great tribulation. There will be intense pressure on the whole church all around the world. Daniel, who speaks of this in terms of seven years (a short period of time), indicates that the difficulties of the second half of that period will be much more severe than those of the first half. We see that represented and confirmed here. The Gentiles (meaning unbelievers) will trample on the holy city (meaning the church) for 42 months (the second half of the seven years of the tribulation).

To some extent the church is always being trampled on: by society's attitude in one place, by actual persecution in another place. For a short time at the end, this will become a severe and universal opposition. So what does the church do? "And I will give power to my two witnesses, and they will prophesy for 1,260 days, clothed in sackcloth" (11:3). Some have suggested that these two witnesses are Moses and Elijah, who literally return to the earth near the end. The later verses in chapter 11 are then interpreted as a renewal of their earlier ministry.

However, the temple and the holy city symbolize the church; the two witnesses could also symbolize something to be understood in terms of the church, and there are specific reasons for claiming this:

a.   The church is to be a witness at all times.

b.   The theme of "two witnesses" occurs several times in the Old and New Testaments – where two witnesses agree, a truth is confirmed (see, for example, Deuteronomy 17:6; Matthew 18:16; 2 Corinthians 13:1).

c.   Jesus sent out his disciples in twos to witness to the kingdom of God (Luke 10:1).

d.   The reference to two olive trees and two lampstands (verse 4) reflects what we read in Zechariah (4:12), where the two olive trees and two gold pipes represent two who are anointed to serve the Lord of all the earth.

e.   In Revelation chapter 1, lampstands represent the churches.

It is therefore possible to interpret these two witnesses as the ministry and mission of the church.

Power is given to the two witnesses for 1,260 days, which again is three-and-a-half years. Why does John switch from 42 months to 1,260 days? It's a mystery!

During the time of the great tribulation, the two witnesses are given power and prophetic ministry. This tells us that the church is not silenced during the tribulation; rather, she speaks with courage and power, and the gospel continues to spread throughout the earth. The power of these witnesses is symbolized by the fire that comes from their mouths: it will destroy enemies, shut up the heavens and bring plagues. The church will not be silent during the great tribulation – indeed in the midst of pressure she will minister with supernatural power. Is that not always true?

Again and again, we hear stories from nations like China, where the church, in the midst of terrible conflict, operates with great power, signs and wonders.

Similarly, in the great tribulation we can expect enormous pressure on the church, with suffering, imprisonment and martyrdom. But there will also be works of power done by the people of God.

This conflict continues, the chapter suggests, to a point where it may seem that the church has lost. In fact even now, in the UK, many people probably think that the church has already lost. But Christians in living and growing churches know that there is another, almost a secret, story.

During the time of the great tribulation, the attack on the church will be led by the Antichrist, introduced as the Beast in verse 7. In Revelation 13 we will read much more about this Beast. Suddenly, near the very end, he seems to have won. The two witnesses lie dead in the street: "Their bodies will lie in the street of the great city, which is figuratively called Sodom and Egypt, where also their Lord was crucified" (11:8). That is a strange verse and needs explanation. The great city represents a worldwide system of unbelief and rebellion against God; it is figuratively called Sodom and Egypt – although Sodom was not a great city and Egypt not even a city.

However, Sodom was a city known for its depravity, and Egypt is represented in Scripture as showing a stiff-necked resistance to God. This is the attitude of the world's system, depraved and stiff-necked in its rebellion. Such a system opposes and attacks the church.

The church at last seems to be overwhelmed, lying dead in the street – and the world has a party. "The inhabitants of the earth will gloat over them and will celebrate by sending each other gifts, because these two prophets had tormented those who live on earth" (11:10). However, just as with Christ, after only a few days there is a mighty and triumphant resurrection, and suddenly the church's position is reversed. "But after three and a half days a breath of life from God entered them, and they stood on their feet" (11:11). It has always been like that; the church is written off as dead and finished – but she lives! It will be like that even in the great tribulation. And now, as John receives more revelation, judgement begins to fall upon the earth.

The victory of God

At last we come to the blowing of the seventh trumpet (11:15). There is a noise in heaven, in distinct contrast to the silence in heaven when the seventh seal was opened. That, of course, was rather tantalizing. All those judgements that come with the opening of six seals are followed by an assurance of the church's security; but then, when the seventh seal is broken and we are all expectation, there is only silence! We are left tingling with anticipation right at the climax.

The first six trumpets have each described judgements on the earth. We have then been given a highly symbolic picture of the church in conflict. As the seventh trumpet is blown, there is noise in heaven. This time we are not kept in suspense. Here, at last, is the victory of God. There is not much detail here (that will come later), but there is enough to confirm to us the final destination of history. "The seventh angel sounded his trumpet, and there were loud voices in heaven, which said: 'The kingdom of the world has become the kingdom of our Lord and of his Christ, and he will reign for ever and ever'" (11:15).

We see around us natural disasters, demonic onslaughts, plagues and conflicts, AIDS and war. There is trouble and pressure for the church, even before the great tribulation. Is that it? Will it just get worse and worse with no real hope, until the world either peters out or blows up?

No!

There is a seventh trumpet. God's sovereignty over all things will be revealed. Everything will be transformed. This world will become the place of God's rule for ever. The kingdom will have come as God establishes his government upon the earth.

There will be no more disasters, no more demons, no more conflicts, no more pain, genocide or death.

The seventh trumpet sounds and Christ will reign for ever and ever.

No wonder the 24 elders begin worshipping (11:16)! It is a time for worship, but also a time for judgement, with rewards for the saints and destruction for the enemies of God (verse 18).

The passage finishes as the temple of God stands open in heaven and John sees the ark of the covenant – that wonderful symbol indicating that God cannot fail to fulfil every one of his promises.

CHAPTER ELEVEN

THE DEVIL
Revelation 12

In the town of Angers, in the Loire district of France, there is a museum that is home to the largest tapestry in the world. Completed more than 600 years ago and woven on to more than 70 separate panels, its detail and colour remain stunning. Peoples of past centuries, not realizing that this was such a wonderful treasure, used parts of the tapestry as carpets and horse covers. Yet, remarkably, most of it remains intact. It is known as the Tapestry of the Apocalypse and it tells the story of the book of Revelation in pictures. It may look rather quaint to us today, but it underlines the value of this book to people who undertook such a mammoth project over 600 years ago.

After chapters that deal with the seven seals and then the seven trumpets, we might expect to move on immediately to the seven bowls of wrath, but instead there is now a section covering three chapters that gives us a fuller picture of the church in conflict. These chapters speak of the Lamb, the Beast and the Devil.

In the twelfth chapter of Revelation we read of the Devil.

The Devil's attack

The first few verses of this chapter speak of the woman, the Son and the Devil. We need to say something briefly about each of these.

Apart from the millennium issue in chapter 20, probably nothing is so debated as the identity of the woman (verse 1). Let me give a flavour of the debate in two quotations:

"Who else can she be but Mary, the mother who gave birth to Jesus?", and "What follows in this vision confirms that this woman symbolizes the church of God."

So some see the woman as Mary, and some see her as the church.

The argument that the woman is a picture of the church can be stated negatively from verse 1, where the description given may initially seem to be a highly idealized picture of Mary: she is clothed with the sun, with the moon under her feet and wears a crown of twelve stars.

However, the church too has a certain glory, and the fact that the woman is clothed with the sun could represent that. The church also has authority, which could be represented by the moon under her feet. Finally, the church is going to reign, and the twelve stars on her head could symbolize that.

The church is also described in other parts of Scripture as a woman. One day, she will be the bride of Christ. We read, "the Jerusalem that is above is free, and she is our mother" (Galatians 4:26). Then in Revelation (21:2), the new Jerusalem (the church) descends, beautifully dressed, as the bride of the Lamb. Also, the woman goes off into the desert for three-and-a-half years, which again is not true of Mary but is true, in a certain sense, of the church, as we shall see later.

But take another look. The woman is pregnant and cries out in pain. She is about to give birth to a male child, who is then snatched up to the throne of God. He will rule the nations with an iron sceptre. This seems to be a description of Mary giving birth to Jesus.

It is a complex picture and its interpretation does depend on how you look at it. Sometimes we seem to see the church, and sometimes Mary, in one and the same woman.

Clearly, the language is highly symbolic.

We also read of the Devil, or Satan. He is described as an enormous red dragon with seven heads, ten horns and seven crowns. There is no question that this is the Devil, for he is named as such in verse 9.

Some have questioned whether the Son in verse 5 is Jesus, because we move instantly from his birth to his ascension. There is no mention of his ministry on the earth, or even his death and resurrection; the Son is born and then immediately snatched up to the throne of God. But we need to realize that John is describing the attack of the Devil, who seeks to destroy Jesus even at birth; but Jesus escapes from Satan to reign from the throne.

There are two points to note from this rather unusual picture.

Firstly, we are warned against being sentimental about the Christmas story. We are familiar with the picture of the newborn baby, the shepherds and the wise men. But we should remember that Mary was really pregnant and had to suffer the discomfort of travelling on the back of an animal while at full term. She ends up in a humble stable and gives birth in real physical pain. And at that point the Devil is there, trying to destroy the baby. We do not receive Christmas cards with a manger and the Devil on them, but this would not be inappropriate! King Herod issued a decree that all babies were to be put to death, and this led Joseph to flee to Egypt with Mary and Jesus. This was Satan's determined effort to kill Jesus right at the beginning of his life. Herod was the human face of these murderous intentions.

This is certainly a reminder that our battle is not against flesh and blood. Our enemies may often seem to be flesh and blood – they may have human faces – but behind evil events there are dark spiritual powers, utterly opposed to the work of God.

Secondly, Stephen Hawking, the severely disabled author of *A Brief History of Time* who is sometimes described as the greatest intellect of the 20th century, was once interviewed about his motor neuron disease. In his reply (only possible because of computer technology), he compared his minuscule suffering and frailty to the immensity of the universe. Because of that comparison, his illness somehow seemed not to matter. That illustrates perfectly why we should study Revelation. We are so often dominated by the minor events of our lives. The really trivial can so easily upset us. If another driver cuts me up, I find myself immediately plotting my revenge! On a more serious note, we can face serious illness, or unemployment, or family tragedy. These things are real and they dominate our thinking. But when we look at Revelation, we see that our lives are played out against a vast backdrop. Our little lives (and they are all little) take place against the background of truly cosmic events.

In history the small and the great come and go. The word of God is at times neglected, and even abused. But there are great cosmic events taking place. The Son reigns from the throne. As Christians, we should always look up: there is always a bigger picture than the events of any of our lives.

The Son of God was born to a woman in physical pain. He was attacked at birth with murderous intent. But in the purposes of God he ministered on the earth, then died and rose again and ascended to heaven. He now rules from the throne of God over all history and for all time; he rules the nations and certainly rules over every detail of our lives.

Victory over the Devil

In this chapter there seems to be some reference to Satan's rebellion in heaven (verse 7). Michael, the archangel and leader of heaven's armies, engages Satan and casts down him and his angels (verse 9). As a result of this, the earth becomes the sphere of Satan's operations and therefore the church and individual believers become the centre of his focus. This is certainly in line with what is hinted at in the Old Testament:

> How you have fallen from heaven,
>   O morning star, son of the dawn!
> You have been cast down to the earth,
>   you who once laid low the nations!

You said in your heart,
 "I will ascend to heaven;
I will raise my throne
 above the stars of God;
I will sit enthroned on the mount of assembly,
 on the utmost heights of the sacred mountain.
I will ascend above the tops of the clouds;
 I will make myself like the Most High."
But you are brought down to the grave,
 to the depths of the pit. (Isaaiah 14:12–15).

However, the emphasis of this passage in Revelation is the defeat of Satan by the work of Christ and the results of this for believers. "They overcame him by the blood of the Lamb and by the word of their testimony" (verse 11). There is something vital and practical here to help us in our lives as Christians.

Authority

"Now have come the salvation and the power and the kingdom of our God" (verse 10). We are in the sphere of Christ's authority. There is a ruler over all rulers and an authority above all authorities. In a dispute you go to an authority. We need, and have, the best possible authority – the authority of Christ.

Accusation

There is an accuser of the brothers (verse 10). Accusation is a common problem for us. We can be told that we're no good, that we've lost it, that we won't even make it on earth, let alone to heaven. There is an accuser, but he has been hurled down. Now we are under the authority of Christ. Paul makes it clear in Romans 8 that nothing, not even demons, can separate us from the love of God in Christ.

Action

There has been action in the shedding of the blood of the Lamb. The blood of Jesus is often the way the Bible speaks of his death.

In Romans (3:25) we read that we are saved by faith in his blood, not faith in his death. Why is this? When we speak of the blood of Christ we are not just saying that Jesus died, but that he gave his life for our life. His life was given for us in the shedding of his blood. That action is the ground of our confidence in the face of accusation. In Revelation 7, we read of the righteous dead who have washed their robes in the blood of the Lamb. The way to be clean before God, and therefore the way to be confident before God, is to believe in the one who shed his blood. He gave his life for our life. All our confidence is grounded there.

> When Satan tempts me to despair,
> And tells me of the guilt within,
> Upward I look, and see Him there
> Who made an end of all my sin.
> Because the sinless Saviour died,
> My sinful soul is counted free;
> For God the Just is satisfied
> To look on Him, and pardon me.
>
> Charitie Lees Bancroft

Application

The shed blood of Christ gives me the ground of my confidence. But we need to apply it by the word of our testimony. Testimony is the truth that we proclaim. In times of pressure or accusation, we can declare that there is no condemnation for us.

Advantage

In verse 11 we read that "they did not love their lives so much as to shrink from death." This is a negative way of saying that we persevere in our testimony despite persecution and accusation, and are even prepared to face the possibility of death. This is our advantage, as those who overcome; we no longer cling to this life so desperately. The suffering of Christians is not a sign of Satan's victory over the saints, but rather of the saints' victory over Satan; for when we suffer, we overcome by the blood of the Lamb.

The fury of the Devil

The last part of the chapter is introduced in verse 12: "He [Satan] is filled with fury, because he knows that his time is short."

Some have suggested that Satan fights so hard against us because he is ignorant of his final destruction and still thinks that he can win. But the Bible presents Satan as one who knows that he has only a little time left, and rages with all the madness of defeat. This is given in picture form in these last verses. We have already read of the woman in the desert, and here we see her again, described in rather difficult symbolic language.

The woman represents the church at this point, and the desert would be her place in the world. "1,260 days" (verse 6) and "time, times and half a time" (verse 14) both equal three-and-a-half years; this is the Bible's picture of a severe time of persecution for the church.

The serpent spews out water against the woman, which would be like Satan spitting in hatred against the church. But the earth helps, and swallows the water. In Numbers (16:31–34), we read of those who opposed the work of God in Moses: the earth opened and swallowed them. Here too we see that attacks on the work of God can be destroyed in this way.

Attacks still take place – verse 17 indicates that sometimes the attack is on the woman, and sometimes on the church as a whole. Sometimes Satan fails in his strategy, and simply tries to pick off individual believers. Scripture is consistent on this matter; whether we are reading Revelation 12 or Ephesians 6, we have an enemy. The Christian life is not *like* a battle, it *is* a battle. Ephesians 6 tells us that there are evil days – times of special attack and onslaught – and so we have to be strong, stand firm, and put on the whole armour of God. But Satan spits at the church and makes war against believers, which is why we have setbacks in the church and, of course, personal difficulties.

Despite the present fury of Satan against us, we can see two real encouragements here.

Firstly, sometimes the earth opens up! This is the language of Revelation, but even on earth we do not endure the fury of Satan all the time, without respite, or, indeed, success. We do get some help. In times of persecution, although there are martyrdoms, there are also supernatural deliverances. There are enough martyrs to remind us that the battle is a real one, but enough supernatural deliverances to give believers the confidence that God is fighting for us. We have already mentioned that during one and the same persecution James was beheaded and Peter was delivered from prison.

There is a tension in church life. Sometimes we wonder why God does not send us revival. We can also wonder, at times, how we have survived at all! We are involved in a real battle; but sometimes the earth opens up and God sends us his help.

Secondly, we come full circle. Our lives, our struggles, the demands of building our little church, are all set against the background of a great cosmic work. We see it here in Revelation. Satan rebelled and was thrown out of heaven. He tried to destroy Christ at birth, and then later, at the cross, he thought that he had won. But Christ escaped him and then crushed him; Christ has ascended to glory, and now he reigns and rules over all the nations. While Satan condemns and accuses, Jesus justifies and releases. God has initiated his plans – plans which are truly cosmic in scope – they cannot fail to come to fruition. The blood of Christ has been shed. His life has been given for our life. We are now under a new authority. We are not defeated in this battle. We overcome by the blood of the Lamb and the word of our testimony.

CHAPTER TWELVE

THE ANTICHRIST
Revelation 13

Many Christians find any discussion of the Antichrist fascinating. A huge amount of speculative, even sensational teaching has arisen around Revelation 13. We therefore need to be as faithful to Scripture on this subject as any other.

Who or what is the Antichrist?

The Bible uses three terms, or names, to refer to the same person. Paul speaks of "the man of lawlessness" (2 Thessalonians 2:3); John speaks of "the antichrist" (1 John 2:18), and in the book of Revelation we read of "the beast". "Antichrist" tends to be the most commonly used term.

We usually interpret the prefix "anti" to mean "against". But in the Greek language, "anti" usually means "instead of". This prefix therefore tells us, not that he is against Christ (which, however, he is), but that he seeks to replace Christ; to be "instead of Christ". Some interpret the Antichrist as a person; others consider that the word could refer to a government or state.

This question cannot really be settled from Revelation 13 alone. It is true that this passage seems to speak of an individual: there are people who follow him and worship him. Also, he speaks, blasphemes, makes war, and recovers from a seemingly fatal wound. However, as we have already seen, Revelation uses highly symbolic language. It would therefore be possible to argue that the Beast of Revelation 13 is a symbol of a state machine, or of a government, that seeks to become everything to everyone, and to take total control over people's lives, even in the area of worship. In this way, the state becomes the Antichrist.

It is thus important to consider the whole teaching of Scripture on this matter, and I would argue that the Bible portrays the Antichrist as an individual. He seems to be prefigured as an individual in the Old Testament: "The king will do as he pleases. He will exalt and magnify himself above every god and will say unheard-of things against the God of gods. He will be successful until the time of wrath is completed, for what has been determined must take place" (Daniel 11:36).

In Mark (13:14), the well-attested variant reading of "he" rather than "it" for the "abomination of desolation" means that the verse reads like this: "When you see the abomination that causes desolation standing where *he* does not belong – let the reader understand – then let those who are in Judea flee to the mountains." This very unusual expression could again point to a personal Antichrist.

This should be compared with the words of Paul: "Don't let anyone deceive you in any way, for that day will not come until the rebellion occurs and the man of lawlessness is revealed, the man doomed to destruction. He will oppose and will exalt himself over everything that is called God or is worshipped, so that he sets himself up in God's temple, proclaiming himself to be God" (2 Thessalonians 2:3–4).

John writes: "Dear children, this is the last hour; and as you have heard that the antichrist is coming, even now many antichrists have come" (1 John 2:18). This verse suggests that there is always a *spirit* of Antichrist in the world (confirmed by 1 John 4:3) but that *the* Antichrist is still to come.

Reading on into Revelation 17, the Beast is distinguished from the city; the latter seems to represent worldly power invested in a state or government.

All of this seems to suggest an individual rather than a state, but there is also an argument from history. At one level, Revelation reflects what was happening to Christians in John's own time. There had been terrible persecution of believers during the reign of the emperor Nero, and now, during the time of the writing of this book (probably in the reign of the emperor Domitian), they were being persecuted again. Such events fit the kind of descriptions given in this chapter.

But throughout history there have been leaders like these, who have ruled with great power and iron authority. They tend to persecute believers, and demand total loyalty and an adoration akin to worship. This is why John says in his letters that such a spirit is already in the world, and it has repeatedly surfaced in individuals across the centuries.

So the Bible seems to teach that although the spirit of Antichrist can be discerned throughout history, *the* Antichrist is still to come in the future. Whatever the system of government may be, it will be led by an individual that Revelation 13 calls the Beast.

Some may still feel that the spirit of Antichrist should be seen as a system of government. But wherever there is such a system, it is always led by an individual. The two are inseparable. A king is powerless without his kingdom, and a kingdom without a king is inconceivable.

The reign of the Antichrist

We now need to ask how the Antichrist manages to reach a position of such authority in the world. In the previous chapter, we saw that Michael cast Satan out of heaven, and that we can overcome him by the blood of the Lamb and the word of our testimony. But in mad, spitting rage, Satan still makes war on the church, knowing that the time to his final destruction is short.

The beginning of chapter 13 is full of threat and malice: "And the dragon stood on the shore of the sea. And I saw a beast coming out of the sea." The picture here is quite deliberately drawn.

Both the Devil (in chapter 12) and the Beast (here in chapter 13) are described in similar ways, as having seven heads, ten horns and several crowns. The Antichrist, or Beast, arises from the sea, but behind him is the Devil. He brings the Beast to prominence and pulls the strings. Behind the visible person of the Antichrist will be an invisible spirit who is the Devil.

In the Old Testament, there are verses that speak of the raging and uproar of the nations as being like a wild sea. For the Jews, the sea was something to be viewed with real fear, so this verse may suggest that the nations will be in great turmoil, with crime out of control and economies collapsing, so that a climate of fear creates the opportunity for the Antichrist to arise and take power.

This is not empty speculation, for just this kind of event is seen in history. The German nation after the first world war was a nation on its knees. The economy was in ruins, inflation was out of control and people could find no jobs. The country was in a terrible state. Suddenly, the Germans seemed to discover their saviour, for, in the midst of the chaos, Hitler came to power. Initially, he seemed to have saved the nation. The economy was restored, people were back at work, and a sense of national pride was recovered as, under Hitler's leadership, Germany began to exercise dominance and authority over other European nations. But for those with eyes to see, this apparent saviour was a devil; the spirit of Antichrist was at work.

With this example in mind, we can imagine a similar sequence of events, occurring this time on a global scale. If the nations are in chaos and economies in disarray, the tendency will be to look for a strong leader to sort out the mess. People will look for a saviour.

The Bible describes the Antichrist as ruling with great authority and power (verse 2). He will establish peace (verse 4) for who can make war on the Beast? He appears to have a supernatural quality, for he receives a fatal wound and yet lives (verses 3, 12).

Some have suggested that this refers to the fatal wound that the Devil received through the work of Jesus on the cross. However, the Devil still lives to persecute the church. If we take this reference literally as referring to the Antichrist, it is interesting again to note that people with the spirit of Antichrist do seem to survive assassination attempts. If that happens, it becomes easier for such individuals to think that they are almost immortal, and for other people to feel that they have some kind of supernatural aura.

The Antichrist will control commerce and finance (verse 17). If you control the financial system, you are also in a strong position to exert political control.

To most people in the world, initially at least, this will look good and reassuring; a strong leader is in control at last. We should not imagine that the rule of the Antichrist will be one of anarchy – far from it. Rather, there will be totalitarian control, with strong, charismatic leadership bringing peace and economic stability. So we read also, "The whole world was astonished and followed the beast" (verse 3). This individual will seem to be a saviour, worthy of being followed. Actually, he will be the Devil incarnate. But such leaders attract worship: "All inhabitants of the earth will worship the beast" (verse 8).

From the word of God we see what happens to individuals (or governments) who possess the spirit of Antichrist. They become obsessed with the need for loyalty, and impose conformity to ensure that it is demonstrated. Verses 11–12 describe a second beast (the False Prophet), who "exercised all the authority of the first beast on his behalf, and made the earth and its inhabitants worship the first beast". He will create a propaganda machine in order to exalt the Antichrist; this will set up his image (verse 14). It is typical of totalitarian leaders that their pictures are displayed everywhere, and that crowds are assembled to hear them when they speak – just as people everywhere will fanatically adore the Beast. Such leaders demand absolute loyalty.

The display of loyalty will be compulsory. This is the meaning of verses 16–17, where we read that everyone had to receive the mark of the Beast. In John's own time, the persecuting Roman emperors demanded a document called a "libellus" as a mark of conformity. To obtain such a document, an individual would need to go to a temple, sprinkle incense into a sacrificial flame and proclaim, "Caesar is lord." The person would then be given the libellus, which testified to his declaration with his signature, witnessed by that of a magistrate.

In the same way, the Antichrist will demand absolute loyalty, and this will be displayed by receiving his mark. Anyone without this mark will be in big trouble. And that is the problem, and always has been for the church. Early Christians would not say, "Caesar is lord", for only Jesus deserves that title. No true believer will be prepared to receive the mark of the Beast, and this will lead to great difficulty for the church in what is called the great tribulation.

There has been, and is, a huge amount of speculation about the nature of this mark, that is often sensational and unhelpful. Revelation tells us only that without it we will be unable to buy or sell (verse 17).

We can summarize this passage by saying that this person, who seems to be the saviour, will prove to be the Devil incarnate – the Antichrist – the "instead of Christ".

Counterfeits

The Antichrist is a counterfeit Christ. Satan is a deceiver – a liar and the father of lies (John 8:44). Therefore counterfeit and deceit mark his kingdom and rule, and he imitates many aspects of our life in Christ with God.

The counterfeit of the Trinity of Father, Son and Holy Spirit is the Devil, the Antichrist and the False Prophet.

There is a counterfeit resurrection. Whatever the precise meaning of the wound that the Beast receives, it is a fatal wound that is healed. The counterfeit lies in the fact that the wound really is fatal, and yet the Beast is still able to deceive the world. There are counterfeit signs and wonders, for John says of the False Prophet, "And he performed great and miraculous signs, even causing fire to come down from heaven to earth in full view of men" (verse 13). There is a reminder here of the authentic prophetic ministry of Elijah. Paul agrees with all this with his statement in 2 Thessalonians 2:9: "The coming of the lawless one will be in accordance with the work of Satan displayed in all kinds of counterfeit miracles, signs and wonders."

Indeed, the False Prophet also plays a counterfeit role. He points people to the Antichrist, just as John the Baptist pointed people to the true Christ (Matthew 3:11).

There is also a counterfeit seal. In Revelation 14, verse 1 we read of the 144,000 who have the Lamb's name and his Father's name written on their foreheads. This seems to reflect the sealing of the 144,000 in chapter 7. But the mark of the Beast is a counterfeit seal, giving a false sense of security because only with it can anyone buy or sell.

This mark is given the number 666. In order to understand this, we need to realize that in the Greek and Hebrew languages, letters carry a numerical value (1 for alpha, 2 for beta etc). Although not mentioned in the Bible, the numerical value of the name of Jesus adds up to 888. So whose name would add up to the number 666? There was a Greek game called Gematria, the goal of which was to find the name behind any given number. My own view is that many people today still try and play the game, but are unable to come up with the name because, as verse 18 says, it is simply "man's number". Depending on each individual's ingenuity and credulity, the number 666 can be worked out to mean almost anything one wishes. It is not surprising therefore that the pope, Martin Luther, John Wesley and many others have been calculated to be the Antichrist. But if this is called man's number, rather than fruitlessly trying to play the game, we should see that *a man* will seek to rule the world. He will exercise great power and authority. However, he is still only a man.

Satan's kingdom is a counterfeit, he gives a false seal, and those who follow him will live in false security.

Overcomers

The book of Revelation is about the victory of God. It is not intended to depress us! Yes, there will be an Antichrist, but there is another side to the story. We can overcome the Antichrist. But how?

Note the warnings

In the Bible, warnings are given to us; this demonstrates the grace of God. Jesus himself warns of the great tribulation, of persecutions, counterfeit signs and miracles, false prophets and false Christs: "Be on your guard; I have told you everything ahead of time" (Mark 13:23). This is why we need to take note of Revelation 13. We are receiving a warning ahead of the event. We need to be on our guard, remembering that we have an enemy.

The time of trouble will be short

The timespan given in this chapter (verse 5) is 42 months (three-and-a-half years). The better-known figure of seven years comes from the book of Daniel. But the tribulation is in two halves. In the first three-and-a-half years, the Antichrist will be establishing himself, and, although there will be warnings, the pressure on the church will not be too severe. In the second half of this period, the Antichrist will be established, and persecution of believers will be universal and intense. But three-and-a-half years probably symbolizes a short period of time.

In Mark 13:20, Jesus specifically says that God has cut short those days. We will therefore be able to help each other to overcome by encouraging one another with the reminder that God will intervene to shorten our sufferings.

> If anyone is to go into captivity,
> into captivity he will go.
> If anyone is to be killed with the sword,
> with the sword he will be killed.

> This calls for patient endurance and faithfulness on the part of the saints. (verse 10).

There will be imprisonment and martyrdom, and this will tax the faith and patience of all believers. But the end is near. Christ is coming back. We will all be with him very soon. The martyrs, of course, will be with him even more quickly!

Spiritual security

"All inhabitants of the earth will worship the beast – all whose names have not been written in the book of life belonging to the Lamb that was slain from the creation of the world" (verse 8).

Our salvation is a settled issue – it's in the book. This is a great comfort for those caught up in the great tribulation. When Revelation speaks of Christ "slain from the creation of the world", we can be encouraged by the fact that Christ's death is effective for all believers whenever they were born, whether before or after the life of Christ.

The end of the story

We read of the coming of the Antichrist in chapter 13, but we will read of the return of the true Christ in chapter 19. He will come riding on a white horse; his robes will be emblazoned with the title: KING OF KINGS AND LORD OF LORDS. He will go to war against the Beast and the False Prophet: "the beast was captured, and with him the false prophet . . . The two of them were thrown alive into the fiery lake of burning sulphur" (19:20). But that is not all! "And the devil, who deceived them, was thrown into the lake of burning sulphur, where the beast and the false prophet had been thrown" (20:10). The counterfeit trinity will be thrown down.

Again, Paul says, "And then the lawless one will be revealed, whom the Lord Jesus will overthrow with the breath of his mouth and destroy by the splendour of his coming" (2 Thessalonians 2:8). We are overcomers because we are united to the Overcomer. We will see the final victory of God and the final destruction of Satan and all his works.

We have to be aware of the Antichrist because we live in this world. History constantly throws up individuals with this spirit. The Bible warns us that there is worse to come. We will see the Antichrist operating on a global scale. The whole world will feel his impact. The Bible gives us a preview of the end times, but Revelation also gives us the better news of what is to come.

The Ancient of Days, the Son of Man, the ascended Christ will arise. He will burst through the heavens and blow away the Devil, the Antichrist and the False Prophet. He is coming for his bride. We are overcomers destined to share the victory of God. And that will last for ever.

CHAPTER THIRTEEN

THE LAMB
Revelation 14

In the previous two chapters we have read descriptions of the work of the Devil and his supreme earthly manifestation, the Antichrist. It is now time for a strong reminder of the victory of God, and that is exactly what we have in Revelation 14. We have had the bad news; now here is the good news.

Although this chapter is headed, "The Lamb", it could have a subheading: "The Most Unoriginal Chapter in the Book"! This part of Revelation is full of material found elsewhere in the book, often down to precise detail.

So, in verse 1, we read of the 144,000 whom we have already met in chapter 7. Also, in verse 8, we read, "Fallen! Fallen is Babylon the Great", which we will see again in chapter 18, verse 2. Why is there so much unoriginal material in this chapter?

We need to remember

How often we hear people complain about their poor memory: "I just can't remember names any more." Equally, we can feel very flattered when people do remember our name.

A look at many magazines and newspapers makes it obvious that there is a whole industry dedicated to helping us with our memories. There are amazing claims made for how quickly we will learn a foreign language if we follow a certain memory technique. Like very many others, I remember where I was when President Kennedy was assassinated, and I remember even more clearly where I was when I heard of Princess Diana's death. We seem to remember these things because they are associated in our minds with certain significant events.

The Bible recognizes how important it is for us to remember certain things, and so it contains many reminders. The Jewish Passover remains an annual reminder of deliverance from slavery. This is carried over into the Lord's Supper with Jesus' instruction, "Do this in remembrance of me." The bread and wine are symbols which remind us of the body and blood of Christ, so that we constantly remember Jesus' crucifixion and the triumph of the cross. For us, as Christians, this is a reminder of our deliverance from the slavery of sin – slavery far worse than that from which the Israelites were delivered. Therefore we remember and we are glad.

We find another example in 1 Corinthians 15:1: "Now, brothers, I want to remind you of the gospel I preached to you, which you received and on which you have taken your stand."

Why do the New Testament writers keep telling us to remember? Because we easily forget. In a world that often seems increasingly hostile to Christian truth and values, we need to be reminded of the eternal perspectives of our faith.

This really is where Revelation 14 fits in. The material here is almost all found elsewhere in this book, but we are being reminded of the facts. Christians can easily say about a Sunday meeting, "Why do we need to come, we've heard it all before?" But long-term experience in pastoral work proves to me that believers often forget – we all need to be reminded.

What should we remember?

There are many great reminders here in Revelation 14.

The security of the people of God

In verse 1, Christ stands on Mount Zion with the 144,000 who have the name of God the Father and the Son on their foreheads. From chapter 7, we have seen that this number is symbolic and speaks of the entire people of God. The seal, or mark, on their foreheads seems to be in deliberate contrast to 666, the number of the Beast, and the mark given to those that follow him.

To be sealed by God is to have our security as the people of God confirmed. It's as though God's people are branded; there is a mark of ownership placed upon them. In the Old Testament – in Isaiah and Micah – Mount Zion is the place of deliverance and glory. As Christians, we are now spiritually on Mount Zion with Christ: delivered, sealed and safe.

The sounds of heaven

We read of the sound of harps and of those that sing a new song (verses 2–3), which again reminds us of what we have already read in chapter 5. But verse 2, with its mention of "the roar of rushing waters and loud peals of thunder" also points us forward to what we will read in chapter 19 as we come to the wedding of the Lamb. Here we are reminded emphatically that heaven will not be quiet! It will be filled with the songs of celebration. There will be new songs declaring that the Lamb is worthy. There will be shouts of "Hallelujah!" so loud that they can be compared only to the sound of vast waterfalls and thunderclaps.

Verses 4 and 5 speak of the purity of the church, which we will return to at the end of this chapter.

The gospel will be preached to every people group

"Then I saw another angel flying in mid-air and he had the eternal gospel to proclaim to those who live on the earth – to every nation, tribe, language and people' (verse 6). But in chapter 5 (verse 9) we have already been told that the blood of Christ will purchase people from every people group on the earth. Verse 6 tells us that the gospel cannot fail to be proclaimed to all the nations. There is no people group among whom Christ will not have a victory, or among whom Christ will fail to build his church.

Today some products are available all over the world. I have drunk Coca-Cola in India and bought a hamburger from McDonald's in Moscow. Companies like these are determined that their logo should be seen everywhere. But the only "company" guaranteed to have its "logo" displayed among every people group on earth is the church of Jesus Christ.

Babylon will fall

Verse 8 proclaims that Babylon is fallen, and indeed Babylon will eventually fall. In chapters 17 and 18, Babylon is seen as a type of all the great world systems that set themselves against God and his church. In our own times, there are worldly systems that seem enormously powerful. They are represented by the media generally (especially television), and by huge financial and marketing institutions and the stock market; all of these can seem like dominating structures in our world. We must be careful not to caricature all this as actively hostile to the church, but it all operates with great power outside the church, and mostly outside the influence of the church.

I sometimes feel this sense of worldly power very strongly when walking among the huge buildings of some great city. Shopping malls can be overwhelmingly big, and some companies seem to wield great economic power. They are influential and can win the affections of a mass of devotees – in some places far more than the church does. There is a great world system. It is powerful and can be very hostile to the things of God.

In the book of Revelation all this is depicted by "Babylon". But great will be its fall. We may belong to a small church that never seems to grow. Babylon looks so powerful and successful. But, remember, we belong to a kingdom that will stand while every other kingdom is shaken to pieces. We belong to a kingdom that will last for ever.

The destruction of God's enemies

Verses 9–11 contain a vivid picture of the destruction of God's enemies. This points ahead to what we will read in chapter 20. Evil is rampant and can appear to have the upper hand. There is clearly an enemy; for example, we see today the extent to which marriages and family life are under attack. But this enemy will be destroyed. God wins. Remember that.

Christians must persevere

"This calls for patient endurance on the part of the saints who obey God's commandments and remain faithful to Jesus" (verse 12).

In the light of so much evil, Christians need to persevere. In the letters to the seven churches, the saints are constantly exhorted to persevere, to be "overcomers" (eg 3:21).

In the face of evil and powerful systems, ungodly attitudes and even persecution, we need to be overcomers, to persevere. That is why we need these reminders. If we realize that a battle is raging, but we feel that the chance of victory is 50/50 or even less, we could say, "What's the point?"

Remember:

● the church will be built
● Babylon will fall
● the enemies of God will be cast down

So keep on going – let us keep persevering.

Dying "in Christ" is gain

"Then I heard a voice from heaven say, 'Write: Blessed are the dead who die in the Lord from now on.'

'Yes,' says the Spirit, 'they will rest from their labour, for their deeds will follow them'" (verse 13). In chapter 11, verse 18, we read, "The time has come for judging the dead." But Paul makes that entirely positive for believers when he says, "For to me, to live is Christ and to die is gain" (Philippians 1:21).

John Chrysostom (c. 347–407, literally, "golden mouthed"), was an outstanding preacher of the early church. He ministered in Antioch and Constantinople, and died after being sent into exile for having displeased Eudoxia, the emperor's wife. His last words were, "To God be the glory in all things." What a way to die! Similarly, John Wesley claimed of the early Methodists that they died well. A Christian does not look forward to a great funeral, but to a great resurrection. We are constantly reminded, by the Scriptures and by observation of our society every day, of one fact: we all have to die. Blessed are those who die in the Lord.

The return of Christ

The book of Revelation touches on this great theme several times, but usually rather mysteriously – we have to read through the symbolism and metaphors. We see that again here, from verse 14, where Jesus is pictured as seated on a cloud, a crown on his head and a sickle in his hand; for he is ready to come and reap a harvest from the earth.

The clearest description of the return of Christ in Revelation comes in chapter 19. There, Jesus is pictured as riding forth on a white horse, and on his robe and on his thigh is written, "KING OF KINGS AND LORD OF LORDS".

Remember: history is not going to peter out. It will reach a climax with the return of the King.

Final judgement

This is described in graphic terms in the last few verses of the chapter (verses 17–20), and picked up with equal definition in chapter 20 (verse 12): "And I saw the dead, great and small, standing before the throne, and books were opened. Another book was opened, which is the book of life. The dead were judged according to what they had done as recorded in the books."

There will be a final judgement for all men and women. Such

a dramatic event requires the dramatic language that we find here, with mention of crushing and a great flow of blood. Although it can sound offensive to modern ears, the Bible does speak of the wrath of God. God's anger will be poured out on his enemies, and they will be cast out of his presence for ever.

We could ask why God allows evil people to continue in the world. One answer would certainly be that he is giving time for people to repent. The appeal of Scripture is for men and women not to show contempt for God's kindness, tolerance and patience (Romans 2:4).

Every one of these truths – God's people are secure, there will be loud sounds in heaven, the gospel will be preached to every people group, Babylon will fall, God's enemies will be destroyed, Christians must persevere, dying in Christ is gain, Jesus will return, we will all finally be judged – is found elsewhere in the book of Revelation. But we so easily forget these important truths, and so we need to be reminded.

Following the Lamb

We now return to verses 4 and 5: "These are those who did not defile themselves with women, for they kept themselves pure. They follow the Lamb wherever he goes. They were purchased from among men and offered as firstfruits to God and the Lamb. No lie was found in their mouths; they are blameless."

We have just seen a symbolic representation of the church in the 144,000. The language continues to be symbolic, otherwise we would have to understand verse 4 as meaning that there are only men in the church! What we have is a symbol of purity, even to the extent that the word "blameless" is used in verse 5. It may seem over-idealized to describe the church as pure and blameless. However, in Hebrews we read, ". . . by one sacrifice he has made perfect for ever, those who are being made holy" (10:14). This verse spans justification and sanctification. Through the sacrifice of Christ at Calvary, the Lamb of God, acting as our substitute, has carried away our sins and guilt. Jesus has done all that is necessary for us to be justified. We are declared righteous in the sight of God.

By that one sacrifice we have been made "perfect" for ever. John the Baptist declared, "Look, the Lamb of God, who takes away the sin of the world!" (John 1:29) Our sin is taken away in its totality. It has been laid on Christ. The sacrifice of Christ makes us perfect in the sight of God. We are now pure and blameless before God – that is justification. However, the same verse (of Hebrews) says that though we have been made perfect for ever, we are being made holy. But, if we are already perfect, how can we also be in the process of being made holy? The answer is that while we are still in this body of flesh, a process is taking place by which we grow more like Jesus. That is sanctification. It means that even now we are being made holy.

But how are we sanctified? There would seem to be no better way of putting it than is done here in Revelation 14:4: "They follow the Lamb wherever he goes." The closer we are to the Lamb, the more our lives will be sanctified and reflect his perfect holiness.

CHAPTER FOURTEEN

FOUR TRUTHS ABOUT GOD
Revelation 15

This is the shortest chapter in the book of Revelation, and introduces the outpouring of the seven bowls of wrath. We will read of these – the third, and last, of the series of sevens – in the next chapter. Here, in Revelation 15, during the worship of the redeemed, we read four truths describing God.

Victorious

Although the seven bowls are the last in the three series of sevens, they cover, once again, the same range of judgements that fall on the earth. In this, the last of the series, we will have a more complete picture of these judgements. One commentator states that "the bowls are last in the order of presentation because they round out the portrayal of divine wrath in seals and trumpets."

Having mentioned these seven last plagues (or bowls of wrath) in verse 1, John once again looks to see the unfolding events in heaven. As in chapter 4, his attention is caught by what looks like a sea of glass: this speaks of the absolute majesty of God. It is as though God is utterly removed and distant from anything we can comprehend, across a sea of glass, in glory and awesome power.

But the amazing truth is that he chooses to have a relationship with us. In this chapter, the sea of glass has the element of fire mixed with it, and in Revelation fire is a symbol of judgement. So we see that the majesty of God includes his judgements. Then again, beside the sea, wonderfully included in the majesty of God, stand those who have been victorious. Our victory always has its source in God. "Victorious" is thus one of those words that rightly belong to God.

Revelation constantly repeats that God is victorious and that we share in his victory. Indeed, as we move towards the end of Revelation there is increasing emphasis on the victory of God. We will read of the fall of Babylon, the return of Christ, the wedding supper of the Lamb, the final judgement and the new heaven and earth. The best is yet to come in this book, so keep reading!

Until now, we have read of war, earthquake, famine, Satan and the success of the Antichrist. It has all been very sobering, but it reflects the realities of this life. However, even before the final chapters of good news, John interrupts earlier passages with reminders of the victory of God, and he does the same thing here.

We are just about to read of the seven bowls of wrath. This is the material of a disaster movie, with sores, fire, earthquakes and Armageddon. But before these crises, we are given a glimpse behind the earthly scene. Beside the sea of glass and fire, and somehow mingled with the majesty and judgements of God, stand those who have been victorious. Even the rule of Antichrist has not caused them to compromise or yield. Some of them may have been martyrs. From the perspective of the world, these martyrs appear to have lost. But actually they stand victorious alongside the majesty of God.

It is important that we don't discard Revelation as a book that is too complicated to understand. This book is exciting! Yes, it has many pictures and symbols. But it tells us what finally happens in this world, culminating in the absolute triumph of God. By the time we reach the last page of Revelation, every prophecy and promise of the Bible will have been fulfilled.

It may not always seem that God is victorious. There are

persecutions and even martyrdoms. In John's time, all of the first apostles, as well as Paul, had been put to death. But John reassures us with the fact that he has seen heaven open and that the conclusion of history has been revealed to him. Men and women of faith are overcomers. They will stand beside the majesty of God and share his triumph. We are in this to win. We don't want to be detached onlookers! However we leave this life and wherever we leave this life, we are here to win and to stand beside the majesty of God.

We can illustrate this with a story from the second world war. Until America entered the war, the Allies had experienced hardly any victories. But when Churchill heard that the Japanese had attacked Pearl Harbour, he knew that it would bring America into the war and declared, "So, we've won at last." At that stage there was nothing to indicate an Allied victory – just the opposite in fact. But Churchill knew that with the might of America on our side it was only a matter of time before the Allies would win.

As Christians, as the church, we have already won! However much we may seem to have lost, whatever struggles may lie ahead, God's victory is certain. We have all the might of God on our side. John looked into an open heaven and saw the final outcome – he knew that the victory of God was inevitable.

Great and marvellous

"Great and marvellous are your deeds, Lord God Almighty" (verse 3).

There are many songs sung in Revelation; this one reflects the song of Moses for the deliverance of the Hebrew slaves from Egypt:

> Who among the gods is like you, O Lord?
> Who is like you –
> majestic in holiness,
> awesome in glory,
> working wonders? (Exodus 15:11)

Just as Moses celebrated the marvellous works of God in delivering his people from bondage, so the people redeemed by Christ celebrate their deliverance, by him, from bondage to sin. Believers are a redeemed people, ransomed by the blood of the Lamb and saved by the mighty works of God. This is certainly worth singing about, and that is exactly what the victorious ones in heaven are doing – "Great and marvellous are your deeds, Lord God Almighty."

True

In verse 3 we read: "Just and true are your ways, King of the ages."

It is vital that we know that God is true, for today believers are engaged in a great battle over truth. I was reminded of this very forcefully on one occasion, when a great deal of public attention was directed towards a pregnant twelve-year-old girl who had been offered help by a Christian charity. This charity was prepared to assist her financially so that she could choose to keep the baby rather than have an abortion. There was a furious response from the so-called pro-choice lobby (which is really not pro-choice, but pro-abortion). The protests were raised because the girl was given a genuine opportunity not to choose an abortion. A particularly low point was reached when, on a public news broadcast, a representative from the charity was asked whether helping a twelve-year-old schoolgirl in this way might encourage other twelve-year-old girls to have sex. One could equally well ask whether offering abortions might not encourage young girls to have sex; but surely the worst aspect of all this is that the question should have been asked at all. It reflects a society that has lost touch with the truth. There are no longer any absolutes, no clear grasp of right and wrong. Tolerance is the religion of our society, where each person decides for themselves what is right.

But, as followers of the Lamb, we fight for the truth. This is not one truth among many, but a single, absolute truth. We stand for *the truth*. God is King of the ages. He lives for ever, and because he is the truth, his truth also lives for ever.

It was Jesus, the Son of God, who made the claim that he is the truth – as well as the way and the life (John 14:6). For those who follow Jesus, everything hinges on that claim. If Jesus is the truth, as he said, then everything he said is true. If not, he would be a liar and everything that he said and claimed would be suspect; every hope that we have in him would fall to the ground. It is as serious as that.

It is worth linking to this the concern that Christians have about what the Bible calls the unforgivable sin, which is identified as blasphemy against the Holy Spirit. The context of this saying can be found in Matthew (12:22–32), where Jesus is accused by the Pharisees of being empowered by Satan when he casts out demons. It is then that Jesus speaks of blasphemy against the Holy Spirit. In context, this blasphemy can be seen as a total reversal of the truth, when Jesus, moving in the power of God, is accused of moving in the power of Satan. God has become the Devil and the Devil has become God. Right becomes wrong and wrong becomes right. This is why a Christian need never be anxious that they may have committed this unforgivable sin. Somebody guilty of such a sin would have reversed all truth and goodness to such an extent that they would no longer have any spiritual awareness or sensitivity.

It seems to me that when it is suggested that help given to a twelve-year-old girl, to enable her to choose not to kill her baby, could encourage other young girls to have sex, we may be dangerously near blasphemy against the Holy Spirit. Everything is being turned on its head; good is being spoken of as evil.

One of the great reasons for defending the Christian message is that it makes sense of life. There is such a battle raging today, for we are called to love people whatever their viewpoint, and yet still hold ourselves to God's absolute truth. Whatever God says is true, because he *is* the truth. We stand on that truth and dare not move off it.

"Just and true are your ways, King of the ages" (verse 3).

Glory

Glory is another of the great words that speak about God. We could understand this either as glory given to God or glory that comes from God. In verse 4 we read: "Who will not fear you, O Lord, and bring glory to your name?" In this case the redeemed are clearly giving glory to God. How do we understand the word "glory"? What actually is glory?

Certainly, we know that it has to do with God. We sing about the glory of God and pray for the glory of God to come to us. But what is it? I warm to the definition of glory as "the shining-out of God". Who and what God is shines out – that is his glory.

Verse 4 speaks of bringing glory to his name. When the question is asked, "Who will not fear [God] and bring glory to [his] name?", the answer must line up with the rest of Scripture. It will be all people, in the sense that people from all races, cultures, colours and languages will bring glory to him. Those from all nations will come and worship the Lord (verse 4).

We have seen this theme before in Revelation. The victory of God means that the redeemed – those drawn from every people group – will finally bring worship to God and the Lamb. In that sense, the victory of God is comprehensive and universal, as people come from all the nations, and worship, celebrating his marvellous deeds and righteous acts. As his quality as the God of the nations increasingly shines out, they will bring God glory.

In our own experience, we discover that the more passionate and heartfelt our worship is, the more God shines out upon us. We bring glory to his name – we state his attributes with joy – and as we do this, we also fulfil something of the prophetic part of this song in heaven.

We have been discussing the glory that we can give to God. But John also experiences the glory that comes from God when, in verse 5, he looks into heaven. He sees what looks like the temple, and out of the temple and, therefore, out from the presence of God, come seven angels who are going to pour out the seven judgements of God. They are the seven bowls of God's wrath that will fall upon the earth. Even as John looks, the temple fills with smoke from the glory of God, and no one is able to enter the temple. This surely recalls the time when Solomon dedicated the first temple in Jerusalem to God; as the glory of God filled the temple on that occasion, not even the priests were able to enter (2 Chronicles 7:1–3).

The glory of God comes – God shines out, and when the glory comes it is tangible, physical and sometimes even visible. Jack Hayford, pastor of Church On The Way in California, tells how the glory of God came down to them during one prayer evening; a silver mist filled their church building. It was an experience that changed his church.

And this is only the introduction to the bowls of wrath!

God is victorious.

He is great and marvellous.

He is true.

He is the God of glory.

Send us your glory, Lord!

CHAPTER FIFTEEN

THE SEVEN BOWLS OF WRATH
Revelation 16

Following the opening of the seven seals and the blowing of the seven trumpets, we now come to the pouring out of the seven bowls of wrath. The bowls of wrath cause events to take place that are parallel to those described when the seals were broken and the trumpets sounded. They describe occurrences across the earth during the whole span of church history.

After the opening of the sixth seal, there is an interlude during which the security of the church is described (chapter 7). With the opening of the seventh seal (in chapter 8), we are left in anticipation of the coming of the kingdom, but the theme is not developed at that point.

After the blowing of the sixth trumpet, there is again an interlude during which a picture is given of the ministry and mission of the church while under great pressure. Then the seventh trumpet is blown, and we reach the climax of history with some details given of the coming of the kingdom.

When the seven bowls are poured out, there is no interlude between the sixth and seventh bowl; instead we are taken right through to the end of history.

Three phrases stand out in this chapter.

Yes, Lord God Almighty

This is the cry of the altar, "Yes, Lord God Almighty, true and just are your judgements" (verse 7). We shouldn't worry too much about a speaking altar! Elsewhere in Revelation the altar is a place of prayer (see 6:10), and the prayers of martyrs and saints are either under or on the altar. Similarly, while we are reading about God's judgements, represented by the bowls of wrath, there comes from the altar a reminder that God's judgements are true and just.

Not only are the three groups of seven parallel to one another; they also seem to indicate a sequence of intensifying judgement. When the fourth seal is opened, one quarter of the earth is affected. When the trumpets are blown, one third of the earth is affected. But when the bowls are poured out, the effect is total. These are not meant to be viewed as precise figures, but they do suggest, not only that God's judgements are poured out in the course of history, but also that those judgements will be intensified.

The first four bowls speak of natural disasters that affect the earth, sea, rivers and the heavens. There seems some reflection here of the plagues of Egypt, for when the third bowl is poured out the rivers turn to blood, as happened to the rivers of Egypt during the time of Moses (Exodus 7:19–21).

When the fifth trumpet was blown (9:1–11) we read a graphic description of the agony and despair of those who put all their trust in worldly systems and philosophies, only to find that they totally failed. This seems now to be intensified, as, with the fifth bowl, God's wrath is poured out on the throne of the Beast. We have already seen that the spirit of Antichrist constantly invades our society. Men and women live without reference to God, but follow lies, falsehoods and other gods. Finally, all this will be shown to be utterly false as God's wrath is poured out. People will be in agony and despair as they see that they have trusted in a lie. As we ponder the moral landslide of our own society, we can discern that this generation is one that has accepted a lie in many areas of life.

There is also a connection between the sixth trumpet and the sixth bowl: both make a reference to the river Euphrates. We saw in an earlier chapter that this river marked Rome's eastern border. It was from this direction that invading armies had often threatened the empire. Here is powerful symbolism: armies and kings who come from across the Euphrates. The sixth trumpet sounds and one third of the human race is killed. But when the sixth bowl is poured out, then, dramatically, we are at Armageddon. There are probably many people who use this term without any idea that it comes in the closing chapters of the Bible. However, all who do use the term probably understand it to refer to a final, cataclysmic disaster.

We know that Armageddon (or Megiddo) was located on the plains of Israel. However, in line with the rather broader interpretation we have given to the seals, trumpets and bowls, we should probably see Armageddon as an event rather than a place. It speaks of a great world conflict before the end.

Now, what has all this got to do with us today? We live in a largely godless and rebellious world. There are many disasters: ships do sink, rivers are polluted, and people do despair of life. These things have touched us all, or at least people that we know. Over the centuries, wars have increased, both in number and severity; in the last century there were two world wars. In the late 1950s, over 30 million people starved to death in China as a result of government mismanagement and coercion. We have seen the horrors of the holocaust, and in recent years there has again been terrible genocide in Africa and Europe. Certainly, the book of Revelation uses pictures and symbols, but these trumpets and bowls represent life as it is, as well as future conflict.

Most people are tempted to think that such events won't happen to them. But in the Bible we find that God often acts "suddenly". Positively, we read, "suddenly . . . from heaven" (Acts 2:2), when the Holy Spirit was poured out on the day of Pentecost. We live with the hope of revival – of another "suddenly from heaven". But "suddenly" can also refer to catastrophes – "While people are saying, 'Peace and safety', destruction will come on them suddenly, as labour pains on a pregnant woman, and they will not escape" (1 Thessalonians 5:3). Jesus too uses the story of Noah, in Matthew (24:36–39), to illustrate the possibility of sudden and unexpected destruction.

There is a pride and arrogance among human beings that causes us to build our structures, set up our programmes, and to do it in our own way, with no reference to God, and with a morality which is designed by our personal convenience. But, suddenly, the stock market can collapse, a natural disaster can fall on us, or an unexpected war breaks out. And there will be an Armageddon for a godless world: a final, great conflict that will affect all humanity.

In this connection, it is important to believe that God's judgements are true and just (verse 7). We always have a tendency to claim that a judgement against us is not fair, and so official judgements are often questioned by an appeal. Such appeals may or may not be justified; however, as this verse tells us, the judgements of God are absolutely true and just.

The Bible is a unity. Revelation is placed at the end, but it is worth going back to the beginning, to the book of Genesis. In chapter 18 of that book, Abraham pleads for the city of Sodom; he makes an appeal against the judgement that God has declared, asking God to spare the city if some righteous people are found there. He asks, "Will not the Judge of all the earth do right?" (Genesis 18:25) Revelation reflects that exactly: "Yes, Lord God Almighty, true and just are your judgements."

Our emotions can cause us to react adversely to the judgements of God, and so our tendency is to say, "It's not fair!" Sometimes we may even be tempted to question the morality of God's judgements. Why should this have happened to him or her or to that particular family? Why should I be unemployed? And so on. But the judge of all the earth will do what is right. He will do absolutely nothing that is unjust. Once again we can say, "Yes, Lord God Almighty, true and just are your judgements."

Blessed is he who stays awake

The idea that Jesus is coming like a thief can be found in the gospels (Matthew 24:42–44), in 1 Thessalonians (5:2) and in 2 Peter (3:10). It is also found here in Revelation 16 (verse 15). "Behold, I come like a thief!" This indicates the unexpectedness of Christ's return. We were once visited by a thief in our home; it was unexpected, and a shock. Verse 15 continues with the suggestion that those who stay awake with their clothes beside them are blessed, because they are ready and will not be caught by surprise. Paul also teaches that Christians will not be caught by surprise at the unexpectedness of Christ's return.

> Now, brothers, about times and dates we do not need to write to you, for you know very well that the day of the Lord will come like a thief in the night. While people are saying, "Peace and safety", destruction will come on them suddenly, as labour pains on a pregnant woman, and they will not escape. But you, brothers, are not in darkness so that this day should surprise you like a thief. You are all sons of the light and sons of the day. We do not belong to the night or to the darkness. (1 Thessalonians 5:1–5)

Christ's coming should not be a surprise to believers. They should have read the signs and be expecting the Lord to return, though not knowing the day or the hour. However, there is more than enough in Scripture to suggest that the Christian needs to keep alert and not to drift off lazily. The emphasis here is on the blessedness of staying awake, and Paul continues in 1 Thessalonians 5, "So then, let us not be like others, who are asleep, but let us be alert and self-controlled" (verse 6). As Christians, we are not meant to settle, becoming sleepy and failing to keep alert.

The New Testament is full of exhortation to move on and advance. Jesus spoke about taking up our cross daily and following him. Paul talks about pressing on towards the prize. If Jesus returned today, would he find us alert, awake and pressing on?

When I returned to a training college where I had spent four years some 30 years previously, I was amazed to find how much was exactly the same. The lecture rooms were unchanged. The student common room was unchanged. The same tables and chairs stood in exactly the same places in an unchanged dining room. They were even serving the same (kind of!) lemon meringue pie. That was in an institution; everything was still much the same. But there should be a sense of progress among the people of God – we should advance towards greater vision, greater faith and increased generosity. We can draw a line and say, "I'm staying this side", but we need to resist settling down; we need to press on, cross the line, and move beyond our current comfort zones.

It is done

The seventh bowl is poured into the air and we are at the very end of history. Revelation now gives us a fuller description of what happens at the end. We will read of the fall of Babylon, the return of Christ, the final judgement, and a new heaven and earth. This book has a wonderful finish! And now, with the seventh bowl, we are at the beginning of the end. There will come a date on the calendar, a time on the clock, which we will be able to read for the last time. Heaven will then declare, "It is done."

In John's gospel, Jesus' last cry on the cross is recorded as, "It is finished" (19:30). The other gospels all say that Jesus cried out in a loud voice. This is an amazing detail. Jesus had agonized in Gethsemane, and probably passed through six trials and interrogations; he had been abused, flogged, crowned with thorns and then brutally crucified; yet he was able to summon a final burst of energy and cry out in a loud voice, "It is finished." In Revelation 16 we read of a loud voice from the throne saying, "It is done!" In both cases, in the midst of what appears to be ruin, disaster and death, these are actually loud cries of victory.

There is a link between those two cries, in that salvation is both individual and cosmic. For the individual, Jesus once prophesied that when lifted up, he would draw all men to himself

(John 12:32). When he was lifted up on the cross, he did all that was necessary to draw to himself all men and women from all the nations, which is why he could cry, "It is finished!" It is a shout of victory; Jesus has died to carry our sin and nothing more needs to be done for any individual.

However, salvation is also cosmic. The work of the cross does not affect only individuals; it is of cosmic proportions. The hints of this were there at the crucifixion, as darkness fell, the curtain of the temple was torn, and an earthquake shook the ground, breaking open the tombs. The crucifixion was not an isolated event in Israel; at that moment, the very universe was being shaken. At the end, we will witness a climax like that.

Hebrews 12:27 tells us that everything that can be shaken will be shaken. We have seen the fall of the Berlin wall, the collapse of Communism, the end of the Soviet Union and the destruction of the World Trade Centre. These are just the little shakings, the minor tremors. But in the end everything will be shaken up, and some things will be shaken down! God can shake the Stock Exchange, the leaders of nations, and even the stars and planets in the sky. Revelation uses pictorial language, but it is highly descriptive. "Then there came flashes of lightning, rumblings, peals of thunder and a severe earthquake" (verse 18), and so it goes on, talking of the collapse of cities, islands fleeing and huge hailstones. But immediately before everything falls to pieces and God seems to have failed disastrously (just as he seemed to have failed when Christ died on the cross), there comes a great shout from the throne: "It is done!" (verse 17). For believers, this is the shout of victory. Is this shaking a disaster? NO! "It is done!" The times are fulfilled, all rebellion is over, pride is finished, worldly systems are at an end and the persecution of the church is swept away. History is complete: It is done.

The book of Revelation is infused with hope, and if we don't see that, we will never understand it. We read of the seven bowls of God's wrath and the threat of Armageddon, but all the time we are waiting for the loud cry, "It is done!" And then Jesus returns – What a story!

CHAPTER SIXTEEN

THE FALL OF BABYLON
Revelation 17 and 18

We should probably understand these two chapters as filling out and expanding some of the details of the seventh bowl of wrath.

Reminding ourselves, once again, that the book of Revelation is about the victory of God, we now read of the final fall and destruction of all worldly power opposed to him. This final disaster is symbolized by the fall of Babylon. In chapter 16 we read, "God remembered Babylon the Great and gave her the cup filled with the wine of the fury of his wrath" (verse 19). We are now given an expanded account of that event.

Chapters 17 and 18 can have a rather overwhelming effect on us. One commentator says, "We may or may not reckon to have grasped the meaning of this long discourse but have we grasped its menace?" In fact, chapter 18 tends to state poetically much of what chapter 17 says in prose. But before going any further, we need to make some introductory comments on Babylon, the woman and the Beast.

Babylon

The first building ever constructed by human beings to challenge the authority of God was on the site of the city of Babylon.

People said to one another, "Come, let us build ourselves a city, with a tower that reaches to the heavens, so that we may make a name for ourselves and not be scattered over the face of the whole earth" (Genesis 11:4). The tallest building in the world was constructed in order that people might make a name for themselves. In recent years, the architect of the twin towers of the World Trade Centre in New York spoke of those buildings as an embodiment and demonstration of the human ability to find greatness. People in their pride always want to make a name for themselves.

But on the site of the original Tower of Babel, as it came to be known, was built the city of Babylon, from where King Nebuchadnezzar exercised his rule. The Babylonian empire became the great enemy of southern Israel; this was demonstrated by the way the armies of Babylon destroyed Jerusalem and the temple in 586 BC. It is thus easy to see how Babylon became a symbol of opposition to God and to his people.

Israel's prophets announced both the restoration of Jerusalem and the ruin of Babylon, and both of these events took place in due course.

In more recent years, Saddam Hussein of Iraq has rebuilt Babylon as a showcase city for parties and entertainment, but not as a place to live. Laser images throw pictures of himself and Nebuchadnezzar on to the clouds above the city.

In the apostle John's day, the Roman empire would have been viewed as the embodiment of the spirit of Babylon, since it opposed the church and persecuted believers. Also, both Babylon and Rome had destroyed the temple at Jerusalem. Today, the spirit of Babylon can be found in worldly structures and government systems that oppose God and the church.

The woman

We also read of a woman who is a prostitute, and who seems somehow to be linked with the city of Babylon. Indeed, reading chapter 17 can be quite confusing. Are we reading about a woman or a city? That question is resolved for us at the end of chapter 17. "The woman you saw is the great city that rules over the kings of the earth" (verse 18). The woman therefore personifies the city and the city is spoken of as a woman. The subtlety of this is brought out in 17:1: "One of the seven angels who had the seven bowls came and said to me, 'Come, I will show you the punishment of the great prostitute, who sits on many waters.'" In Jeremiah (51:13) there is a reference to Babylon as, "You who live beside many waters"; the city was in fact built on the banks of the river Euphrates, and had many irrigation canals. So the prostitute sitting on many waters is a description of Babylon.

This woman causes great astonishment (verse 6) and intoxicates the inhabitants of the earth (verse 2); she is evidently what might be termed a "stunner" or "drop dead gorgeous" – she is glamorous, dressed to kill; she glitters and oozes sex appeal.

Babylon is described like this is because of the city's seductive spirit. Worldly structures and systems can be very seductive. We see this today in our own cities, which are so often places of pride, power and corruption, but yet can be very seductive in their entertainments and opportunities to make money. Even in poorer cities like Mumbai (formerly Bombay) in India, there are people who are able to make fabulous amounts of money. You can have fun in the city, and indulge any appetite, fantasy or craving. The prostitute seems to represent the fact that in the city any pleasure and any vice can be purchased for money. The city is therefore depicted as a highly seductive woman – the great prostitute.

The Beast

We have already read in some detail about the Beast, or Antichrist, in Revelation 13. A spirit of Antichrist is always at work in the world, seeking to usurp the place of Christ. In this chapter, the woman rides on the back of the Beast. So this woman, or Babylon, draws her power, charm and seductiveness from her alliance with the Beast.

Now we are ready to pick out some key themes from these chapters.

The desert

"Then the angel carried me away in the Spirit into a desert" (17:3). Commentators do not agree on the meaning of this statement, but I take it to mean that John is taken into the desert so that he can see things more clearly. The desert is lonely, a place of isolation. There is space to think, and to get things into perspective. In the desert, John is better able to understand the world and its systems that oppose, or seek to replace, God.

We are surrounded by so much that is opposed to godliness and righteousness, and, it seems, increasingly so. One of the clever strategies of such systems is that they give us no space to think and gain a proper perspective on life. When individuals really think things through, they often begin to see the possibility of change and improvement.

Television, with its ever-growing multiplication of channels, is obviously one of the things that crowds and bombards us, giving us no clear space to think. Modern life is filled with frenetic activity and complicated demands. I feel this whenever I have to tap yet another set of pin numbers into machines to gain information, money, or some kind of service. The result is that we end up without time to think. We then need to correct this, by going into the desert to give ourselves some space.

I remember the evangelist David Watson once saying that he was talking to an undertaker while on his way to conduct a funeral. He referred to the fact that the undertaker was dealing with death every day, and asked him what he thought happens when a person dies. This manager of corpses replied that he had never really thought about it!

Our minds are crowded with urgent news poured out by newspapers and televisions day after day. But our minds are also consumed with the little details of daily life, from pin numbers to the football results. Yet we are going to judge the angels one day –

we have some serious issues to think through from a biblical perspective.

It is good to be alone sometimes, to go into the "desert" and think.

The deception

In chapter 13, we saw that the Antichrist system is demonically inspired. The Antichrist will himself be a demonic counterfeit: the Devil made flesh. We see this system expressed throughout history by worldly systems opposed to God, demonic in origin and totally deceptive. We can view this deception in various ways.

It is supernatural

In 17:8 we read of the Beast who "once was, now is not, and [yet] will come". This is the counterfeit of the true and living God, who, in 1:8 is spoken of as the one "who is, and who was, and who is to come". The counterfeit goes as far as an apparent resurrection, for the Beast receives a fatal wound, yet lives. But this has happened throughout history. Satan was defeated at the cross, yet he seems to have made a great recovery, and even now is alive and active against the church. But it is a deception, because he is on his way out. "The beast . . . will . . . go to his destruction." (17:8a) "And the devil, who deceived them, was thrown into the lake of burning sulphur, where the beast and the false prophet had been thrown. They will be tormented day and night for ever and ever" (Revelation 20.10).

It is economic

"The woman was dressed in purple and scarlet, and was glittering with gold, precious stones and pearls" (17:4).

These are the fruits of the woman's trade. In chapter 18 there is a great deal said about the luxuries of Babylon. Cities are the locations of powerful economic systems, described in terms like the City of London, the Stock Exchange and Wall Street. There is a huge economic system, so voracious and so powerful. It is very seductive, for men and women love money. It glitters and it entices. But, "Fallen! Fallen is Babylon the Great!" (18:2) Chapters 17 and 18 make it abundantly clear that all the economic systems of this world will finally crumble. All that people have built their hopes on will collapse.

Hitler boasted that he was building a thousand-year Reich, yet it was destroyed in a war lasting only six years. Rome built a mighty world empire, which now can only be viewed in bits and pieces in museums around the world! Communism at one time controlled the whole of Eastern Europe, but folded like a pack of cards after only 70 years. Our present world "empire" is capitalism with all its seductions. But the whole Babylon system – every system that seeks to replace God – will one day fall.

It is physically seductive

This title was written on her forehead:

MYSTERY
BABYLON THE GREAT
THE MOTHER OF PROSTITUTES
AND OF THE ABOMINATIONS OF THE EARTH. (17:5)

In the city of Rome, prostitutes wore headbands with their name written on them. Prostitutes ply their trade through seduction. Today, much of our entertainment industry sets out to be physically seductive. We live in that kind of world, and this deception confronts us in our everyday life. But Revelation tells us that it too will be judged, and will fall.

It is a seduction to false worship

"I saw that the woman was drunk with the blood of the saints, the blood of those who bore testimony to Jesus" (17:6). This speaks of the attempt of worldly systems to extinguish the church. That was certainly true in the first century; it was happening through direct persecution. The same spirit is at work in the West today, but now it tries to treat the church as an irrelevance. Yet, at the same time, there is a huge growth of interest in "religion", an apparent addiction to horoscopes in almost every magazine, and increased devotion to new age beliefs.

We have already seen that in the days of the Antichrist there will be a particular False Prophet who will call people to worship the Beast. But the spirit of Antichrist is always at work in the world, and so there are always false prophets telling us how we should worship. Any foolishness is trotted out, so long as it distracts people from the one true God. It is a great lie and a great deception.

However, Revelation (17:16) tells us that the prostitute will burn; all her seductiveness will be reduced to ashes.

The defeat

"They will make war against the Lamb, but the Lamb will overcome them because he is Lord of lords and King of kings – and with him will be his called, chosen and faithful followers" (17:14).

War against the Lamb is war against the people of God, for "with him" will be his followers. The church is so identified with Christ, that to come against the Church is to come against Christ. The ascended Christ's question to Paul on the road to Damascus directly implied that Paul was persecuting *him*. Paul was in fact persecuting the church, but the church is the body of Christ, so to persecute her is to persecute Jesus.

What will happen to the church at the end of history? Some have suggested that only a remnant of believers will remain, but that Jesus will arrive back just in time to rescue them. Others suggest quite the opposite and predict a massive end-time revival. The truth is that two things seem to be happening simultaneously as the end approaches. As we have already seen, the gospel will be preached to all peoples; the full number of the Gentiles will come in, and all Israel will be saved (Romans 11:25–26), which probably refers to a massive turning of Jews to Jesus as their Messiah. But there will also be great tribulation, and war will be declared on the church. That is mentioned here in verse 14 where we read of war against the Lamb which, as we have seen, must include his faithful followers.

One fascinating aspect revealed to us here is that finally, the Beast turns against the woman – Satan divides his own house. "The beast and the ten horns you saw will hate the prostitute. They will bring her to ruin and leave her naked; they will eat her flesh and burn her with fire" (17:16).

It is always a battle for those who follow the Lamb, and there will be yet greater battles as Babylon and all that it represents increasingly turns against us. But the Lamb and his followers will overcome. If you have ever made a journey which you considered really dangerous, imagine how total your confidence would have been if, before starting out, you had seen a video recording of your safe arrival! In this journey of life, we have the "video" of the conclusion; it is here in the book of Revelation. The Lamb will overcome; Satan will be defeated – and we can therefore be entirely confident.

The demand

"Then I heard another voice from heaven say: 'Come out of her, my people, so that you will not share in her sins, so that you will not receive any of her plagues'" (18:4).

Seven times in the New Testament there is a demand to "Come out of Babylon!" We have been arguing that Babylon is to be identified with worldly structures and systems hostile to God. Some Christians remain in Babylon, in the sense that they become martyrs in the city. The history of persecution against the church is replete with a strange mixture of much martyrdom and much supernatural deliverance.

We can also say that the demand to come out of Babylon is a challenge to worldly attitudes that, even as believers, we can easily slip into. Believers can be seduced by money, salacious entertainment, luxury, and even the desire to read their horoscopes. There is something very attractive about the systems of this world. However, our attitude should be that it is all going to fall. Babylon will come to ruin; the final victory is with God.

The Bible can be thought of as a "Tale of Two Cities": the story of two women. The two cities are Babylon and Jerusalem. Babylon is the great city of this world, powerful, and opposed to God. Jerusalem is the city of God. This is what we read about Babylon: "Woe! Woe, O great city, O Babylon, city of power! In one hour your doom has come!" (18:10) In contrast, we read about Jerusalem, "I saw the Holy City, the new Jerusalem, coming down out of heaven from God" (Revelation 21:2a). This describes the city of God, which is the church.

Babylon falls down, but the church *comes* down, to live on a new earth, where she will be with Christ for ever.

> Saviour, since of Zion's city
> I, through grace a member am,
> Let the world deride or pity
> I will glory in Thy Name:
>
> Fading is the worldling's pleasure,
> All his boasted pomp and show;
> Solid joys and lasting treasure
> None but Zion's children know.
>
> John Newton

There are two symbolic women, the prostitute and the bride. The prostitute represents the active spirit of the systems of this world. This is what we read about her: "The beast and the ten horns you saw will hate the prostitute. They will bring her to ruin and leave her naked; they will eat her flesh and burn her with fire" (17:16).

But the woman that Jesus loves is his bride. "I saw the Holy City . . . prepared as a bride beautifully dressed for her husband" (21:2). The bride in her beauty personifies Jerusalem, just as the prostitute with her tawdry glitter personifies Babylon. Babylon will fall and the Prostitute will burn, but the church is the city of God and the bride of Christ. She will live and she will reign for ever.

CHAPTER SEVENTEEN

CELEBRATIONS AND THE RETURN OF THE KING
Revelation 19

Many things in the book of Revelation can appear obscure: seals, trumpets and bowls of wrath. All of these speak of judgements that fall upon the earth and bring us to the edge of the eternal age. So far, however, we have only had a number of hints about the end of this age and the eternity to come. But in the closing chapters of the book we now see many details of what is to come in the future.

What is clear from these final chapters is that the place to be at the end of history is "in Christ". We consider three great themes:

● Hallelujah!
● The wedding of the Lamb
● The return of the King

Believers will be on the winning side at the end of history – so it's "Hallelujah!" anyway; we're off to a wedding and Jesus is coming back!

Hallelujah!

In Hebrew, the word "Hallelujah" conveys the sense of "Praise Jehovah" or "Praise our covenant God." But it is an international word; you hear the actual word "Hallelujah" in other languages. Although we read the word many times in the Psalms, we only find it in the New Testament at this point in Revelation.

The beginning of Revelation 19 follows on from the previous two chapters with their description of the fall of Babylon. We now read heaven's response to that event. We have seen that Babylon is the great worldly system opposed to God and the church; Babylon, the spirit of which leads to the persecution of the church; Babylon, full of corruption, greed and vice as personified in the great prostitute. But at the end of history Babylon falls – "Fallen! Fallen is Babylon the Great!" (18:2)

Chapters 17 and 18 have described Babylon's fall from an earthly perspective. Those who have trusted in worldly structures and the seductive spirit of Babylon will be devastated by its fall. Chapter 19 now gives us heaven's perspective. Here, the change of mood could not be greater. Those on earth cry out, "Woe! Woe, O great city" (18:10). But heaven is filled with shouts of "Hallelujah!" at the condemnation of the great prostitute.

The shouts of "Hallelujah!" seem to intensify in the opening verses of this chapter. They begin like the roar of a great multitude. This is then increased when the 24 elders and living creatures cry "Amen, Hallelujah!" Then comes the call for every servant of God to participate in the praise. Finally, the noise is overwhelming. "Then I heard what sounded like a great multitude, like the roar of rushing waters and like loud peals of thunder, shouting: 'Hallelujah! For our Lord God Almighty reigns'" (verse 6). A victory is no time for quiet shouting! Football crowds don't whisper, "It's a goal" – they roar it out. Churches are not meant to be companies of quiet whisperers. In heaven, the shout of "Hallelujah!" celebrating the final fall of Babylon will be at full throttle.

There are two points to note about this victory.

It will deal with every hurt

Sometimes we can be upset by something quite trivial, like a wet bank holiday when we'd planned a day at the beach. But in the body of Christ there is also a great deal of genuine pain. The martyrs cry out from under the altar in heaven, asking how long it will be before their blood is avenged (6:9–10). As we reach the end of history, as recorded in this chapter, we see that God does indeed avenge the blood of his servants (verse 2). There will be a day of vindication for all those who have suffered for the gospel, and specifically for the martyrs. This will not be a time of sadistic revenge, but God, whose judgements are true and just, will judge his enemies and in so doing avenge the blood of his servants.

This also speaks of a wider truth. Some believers walk through life with a great deal of grief and pain, and the cry of their hearts is, "How long?" As a pastor, I have wished many times that I could snap my fingers and set everything right for an individual in pain. There is of course the fellowship, care and prayer of their local church for those who suffer. But in addition to that, we need to declare that one day all will be set right, for God will avenge the blood of his servants. One day, God will bring in a new order. "He will wipe every tear from their eyes. There will be no more death or mourning or crying or pain, for the old order of things has passed away!" (21:4). We cannot set aside every grief and pain today; some will have to wait a little longer. But God will achieve the final victory.

Every enemy will be routed.

Every tear will be wiped away.

We will join the Hallelujah chorus.

It is a victory that will last for ever

I have sometimes been asked what could happen in the future. When Jesus returns and the whole of creation is restored, could man fall into sin again as Adam did, and bring about a new fall and a new cycle of history? That is really a philosophical question, but it is one that the Bible answers. We read, "And again they shouted: 'Hallelujah! The smoke from her goes up for ever and ever.'" The phrase "for ever and ever" conveys the idea of eternity without end. God's great victory will not simply be that every enemy will be destroyed, but that every enemy will be destroyed *permanently*. So, Hallelujah! There is no prospect that sin will ever again rear its ugly head!

The wedding of the Lamb

In the Bible, various images are used to depict the church. Most commonly we read of the body of Christ, but here the term used is "the Bride" (verse 7). In the Old Testament, Israel was spoken of as the wife of God. The prophets, denouncing the apostasy of Israel, spoke of the nation as a faithless wife. Here, however, the church is the bride, and her wedding to Christ is proclaimed amid tumultuous celebrations.

If we use the terminology of marriage, it is probably best to say that the church is *betrothed* to Christ at the present time. In the New Testament period, a betrothal was a legally binding commitment to marriage. It was the status of Mary and Joseph when Mary became pregnant by the Holy Spirit. A betrothal could only be broken by a divorce, which is what Joseph considered until God spoke to him about the true situation.

In Ephesians, the relationship between Christ and the church is likened to that between a husband and wife: "Husbands, love your wives, just as Christ loved the church and gave himself up for her . . . to present her to himself as a radiant church, without stain or wrinkle or any other blemish, but holy and blameless" (Ephesians 5:25–27). The church, which Christ will one day present to himself, will then be his radiant bride. Writing to the church at Corinth, Paul also speaks of the way in which he promised (literally, "betrothed") the church to Christ (2 Corinthians 11:2).

However, in Romans Paul speaks of the believers as already glorified, because it is so certain that it will happen. In the same way, although the church is presently betrothed to Christ, we could argue that she could already be called the bride of Christ, because it is certain that that is what she will, one day, be. Revelation is speaking of that glorious day that is yet to come.

There will be a wedding, when the church and Christ will be joined together, for ever. "Let us rejoice and be glad and give him glory! For the wedding of the Lamb has come, and his bride has made herself ready" (19:7).

Some time ago I attended a secular wedding. The couple were not believers, but they wanted a wedding ceremony, which in fact was structured rather like a Christian wedding service. The bride walked down the aisle to be given away by her father; there were bridesmaids, a best woman (!) and a leader who took the role of what would have been the pastor in a church wedding. Vows and rings were exchanged and there were songs and readings. There was even a congregational song:

> Just a perfect day
> You made me forget myself
> I thought I was someone else
> Someone good.

I realized that this is exactly the opposite to what we will sing at the wedding of the Lamb:

> For the wedding of the Lamb has come
> and his bride has made herself ready.
> Fine linen, bright and clean,
> was given her to wear. (verses 7–8)

The gospel is this: something is given to us. What is given to us is, in fact, goodness, which the Bible here calls righteousness. The bride makes herself ready, in that she repents and believes in Christ, but the reason the bride rejoices and gives God glory is because a righteousness is given to her that allows her to marry Christ.

So often, people live by the myth that an acceptable goodness can be achieved through their own efforts. However, the truth expressed by this modern song captures the insight that, deep down, most people know that they are rotten to the core. You can have a nice day; someone may declare that they love you; you can temporarily feel better about yourself. But what is the real you? The Bible uses terms like "far off" and "dead in our trespasses" to describe us. There is not enough good within any of us to enable us even to live at peace with others, let alone with God.

Here is the great difference. At the end of history there will be a wedding, and every believer will be there. Their attendance will not be *earned* by self-righteousness or because someone has made us feel better about ourselves. It will be guaranteed because "fine linen" has already been given us to wear. God clothes us with righteousness as a free gift. We will appear as the bride of Christ – spotless, clean and radiant.

And what a wedding it will be! Believers will be both the bride and the guests! "Blessed are those who are invited to the wedding supper of the Lamb!" (verse 9). However, we are not just invited; the description points to a full and final union between Christ and his church. The idea of a wedding feast to come is a common theme in the New Testament. We may feel that it is only picture language, but if so, the feast will have something better than food and drink as we know it!

Verse 9 tells us, "These are the true words of God." The whole Bible is the true word of God. But here there is a particular emphasis on the wedding and on the feast.

It is going to happen.

It is absolutely certain.

These are the true words of God.

The return of the King

Finally, in this chapter, we read one of the most dramatic, and certainly one of the most poetic, descriptions of the return of Jesus Christ.

The hints that have been there throughout this book now climax in this great picture of the return of the King. Over 300 times, the Bible tells us that Jesus will come again. It is the crisis to which all history is moving. It will be the great culmination of this present age – an age that will finish, not in a nuclear night, nor through a meteorite strike, nor because a pandemic wipes out the world population. The truth to which the Bible looks, and which has been the Christian hope throughout history, is that the King is coming back.

John now describes this last great event before the start of the new order. Whereas previously John saw a door standing open in heaven, he now sees all heaven standing open before him (verse 11). Dominating the scene, and ready to ride forth as a mighty champion, is a rider seated on a white horse. The name of this rider is Faithful and True, and we know that John is seeing the King ready to ride out to victory.

For all of history, this earth has been the focus of God's interest. The one who now comes again was once born amongst animals in a stable on this earth and entered Jerusalem, in peace, upon a donkey. The same one gave himself up like a lamb to be slaughtered. Now he sits victorious on a white horse, and will ride forth as the King. Every action that this King has performed has been faithful, and every word that he has spoken has been true. This is no gentle Jesus, meek and mild. As God's word says, this is the one who makes war upon his enemies; this is the one who "makes [all] wars cease to the ends of the earth" (Psalm 46:9). This rider is indeed a mighty conqueror.

The eyes of this King are like blazing fire – just as John saw right at the beginning of his vision, when the figure of Christ in glory appeared before him, the sight of which caused John to fall at his feet as though dead. The same eyes that once devastated Peter will blaze and penetrate every human being when the King comes again. This King is crowned with many crowns. Many men and women have worn a crown, and the Beast and the Dragon had several; but this Man wears many crowns, for only he is the Sovereign Lord.

Although he is called Faithful and True, and the Word of God, he also has a name that no one knows but he himself. In the Bible, the name of an individual describes his or her very character and personality. This means that non-believers cannot know the name of Jesus in the sense that he is Saviour, Redeemer, Judge and coming King. We, as believers, look on him whose name we know and honour and worship, yet who in his very essence is more than we can possibly know in this life, where "we see but a poor reflection" (1 Corinthians 13:12).

This King wears a robe dipped in blood; this is the blood of his enemies, symbolizing the certainty that Christ will execute divine wrath, not merely petty anger, upon all his enemies.

One of the Lord's names that is revealed to us here is "the Word of God". God spoke his word, and the whole of creation came into existence. This world was made through Christ and for Christ, who was himself the Word made flesh. People looked on him and saw that he was full of grace and truth, the exact representation of his Father in heaven. What is God like? Well, look at the Word of God. As history comes to an end, the Word of God will finalize all things according to his eternal purpose. But this King does not ride out alone: he comes with the armies of heaven. Angels attend him; we know that they come with Christ in his Father's glory at his return. But the armies dressed in fine, clean and white linen can only refer to the saints of God. Raised from their graves, raptured from the earth, with new, transformed and glorified bodies, clothed in the righteousness purchased for them by the Lord, they too now follow the King of the ages.

He will come to execute final judgement. No man or woman, no earthly king, no world leader, no nation, can escape the destiny of the ages. He will strike down the nations (symbolized by a sharp sword coming out of his mouth); next, he will rule them with an iron sceptre. "The winepress of the fury of the wrath of God Almighty" then speaks of their final judgement.

His name is clearly written so that everyone can read it. This name proclaims his sovereign authority, which immediately reduces, as to nothing, every other authority that has ever exercised power on this earth. This glorious champion is none other than KING OF KINGS AND LORD OF LORDS.

The final defeat of all his enemies is described, as an angel standing in the sun (symbolic of the highest place in the universe) calls together the birds of the air. In some terrible counterpart to the marriage supper of the Lamb, they will devour all his enemies at the great supper of God. This picture of birds eating flesh is used in the Old Testament, where it speaks of the punishment and total defeat of God's enemies. This King will impose his will on all his opponents, and none will be left to rebel against his godly rule.

Wherever rebellion, opposition, arrogance and independence are found; wherever the kingdom of Antichrist and its false prophets so control the minds of people that they have no place for the God of the ages; and wherever materialism and short-term gain are everything, and eternity is regarded as nothing; they will all be cast down and utterly destroyed.

At the end of the ages, his names sound out: Faithful and True, the Word of God, KING OF KINGS AND LORD OF LORDS.

Jesus will return.

"Hallelujah! For our Lord God Almighty reigns."

CHAPTER EIGHTEEN

RESURRECTION AND JUDGEMENT
Revelation 20

The first six verses of this chapter contain one of the most controversial passages in the whole of Scripture. It all has to do with the period of a thousand years; this is mentioned several times, but the most crucial reference is probably in verse 4: "They came to life and reigned with Christ for a thousand years." We need to address three questions to this statement: Who? When? And where?

Who reigns with Christ?

In the broadest sense, all believers reign with Christ, but the emphasis here is on those who have died as Christians.

When do they reign with Christ?

This is a crucial question, and basically two answers are given:

a. They will reign with Christ in the future for a thousand years, after he has returned. This period is sometimes understood literally, and sometimes understood to refer to a long, but indefinite, period of time. This view is known as premillennialism, for Christ returns before his thousand-year (i.e. millennial) reign.

b.   They are reigning now with Christ. The whole church age is symbolized by the thousand-year period, and believers (especially those who have died) reign with Christ for its whole duration. This view is known as a-millennialism.*

Where do they reign with Christ?

Again two answers are given: \

a.   They will reign on the earth with Jesus in the future.
b.   They are reigning in heaven and glory with Jesus now, at the present time.

Where does this leave us?

Does this mean that we are unsure of the correct interpretations here? A problem is created by the fact that different, but brilliant, Bible scholars give conflicting interpretations. Some say that we will reign on the earth with Jesus for a thousand years after he has come again, and that this will be followed by the final judgement and the eternal age. Others say that Jesus reigns with his saints in glory throughout the church age (symbolized by the thousand-year period), and that we are now waiting for the return of Jesus, which will be immediately followed by the final judgement and the eternal age.

Two quotations give a sample of each interpretation:

> To separate chapter 20 from chapter 19 destroys the whole sequence [of the argument]. This is widely done in the interests of the a-millennial and post-millennial positions, who want to make chapter 20 a "recapitulation" of the whole church age and not a sequel to the events of chapter 19. This should be seen as an artificial separation, relying heavily on the medieval chapter divisions. (David Pawson, *When Jesus Returns*, p. 213)

---

* There is a fuller discussion on this subject, including post-millennialism, in my book, *Thinking Clearly: The End Times*, Monarch, 2000.

The New Testament knows of only one Parousia, and that is the "day of the Lord" which will end all things. If this "end" is described in chapter 19, then the thousand years described in chapter 20, even though they follow it in the book, must precede it in actual history; in a word, 20:1–6 is a flashback. The binding of Satan, the first resurrection, and the millennium are all metaphors for the present situation in the world, covering the period between the first and second comings of Christ. (Michael Wilcock, *The Message of Revelation*, p. 179)

I could say at this point that you are fortunate to be reading this book so that I can give you the correct answer!

It is, in fact, possible to make out a good case for both positions.

Some say that we read in Revelation 19 that Jesus returns, and that events then follow one after another in chapter 20. This would mean that after Christ's return, Satan is bound for a thousand years, which would then allow Jesus to reign on the earth with his church during that period. Revelation 20 says that Christ reigns for a thousand years with his people; according to this view, we should just accept what it says.

However, others say that nowhere else does the Bible give us this teaching. Revelation 20 doesn't even say that Christ reigns on the *earth* for a thousand years, just that he reigns – which would be better understood as reigning from heaven. Many other arguments are used on both sides of this debate.

We need to ask, "Does it matter?" The answer, in my opinion, would be, "Not a great deal!" Both viewpoints teach the return of Jesus, the final judgement and the eternal age with a new heaven and earth. The only real difference is whether Jesus spends a thousand years on the earth with his church, or not, before the eternal age. But what is a thousand years in the light of eternity? From this point of view, we can see that it is wrong to make too big an issue out of this. It would be tragic if the many wonderful and clear truths in Revelation 20 were to be obscured because of a dispute over matters of lesser importance.

My own view is that this chapter describes the reign of Christ with his people in glory throughout the church age, and that this is represented by the thousand-year period. I need to state this viewpoint here, because it affects my interpretation of the rest of the chapter.

The binding of Satan

Verses 1–3 tell us that Satan is bound for a thousand years and that during this time he is unable to deceive the nations. I take this to mean that Satan is bound during the whole church age. But is this reasonable? Can we really say that Satan is unable to deceive the nations any more? He appears to be very successful in some nations. In fact, the whole idea that Satan is bound presents us with a challenge throughout the New Testament. "He [Jesus] replied, 'I saw Satan fall like lightning from heaven. I have given you authority to trample on snakes and scorpions and to overcome all the power of the enemy; nothing will harm you.' (Luke 10:18–19). Jesus said those words to his disciples, most of whom would be put to death for their faith. So in what sense is Satan fallen, and in what sense will the disciples remain unharmed? We can compare Paul's words here, "And having disarmed the powers and authorities, he made a public spectacle of them, triumphing over them by the cross" (Colossians 2:15). However, we still have abundant evidence of the activity of demonic powers, and the New Testament speaks a great deal about warfare with Satan.

We can perhaps resolve these difficulties by noting that there is a difference between the defeat of Satan, and his destruction, both of which are mentioned in this chapter. At the cross, Satan was dealt a terminal blow from which he cannot recover. However, defeated enemies sometimes fight back fiercely and this is true of Satan. He is defeated and therefore he will be destroyed. But between the cross and the return of Jesus, he fights with the greatest hatred and ferocity.

In verse 7, we read that at the end of history, Satan will

deceive the nations by making an all-out, concerted attack upon the church. We do not currently experience such an attack, so at present, throughout the church age, Satan is bound. He is restricted, since he does not have control over the nations. The gospel can therefore advance, often taking new ground and reaching into areas that were previously closed to the message of Jesus. Every new convert to Christ is a testimony to Satan's present inability to deceive the nations.

But at present, we need to remember that we are involved in a battle. Demonic forces oppose us – it really is as serious as that. Yet, this is not a war that we will lose. There will be setbacks, but the church will keep advancing. Satan, who is already defeated by the work of the cross, will finally be destroyed.

The reign of the believers

We read of those who will reign with Christ throughout a thousand years (verses 4–6). This is clearly a reference to believers – all interpreters agree about that.

Verse 4 speaks of those given authority to judge. The New Testament reveals this as one of the extraordinary blessings of belonging to Christ. In some way, believers will serve as judges alongside Jesus. It seems that we will even judge the angels (1 Corinthians 6:3). The fact that these believers are described as seated on thrones is particularly significant. The Greek word for "throne" is used 45 times in the book of Revelation, and except for three clear references to the throne of Satan, these thrones are always in heaven. This is therefore a picture of the people of God in heaven.

This part of the chapter helps us to understand the references to a first resurrection and a second death. Christians who die before the return of Christ will be raised to life with him and reign with him in glory. When Jesus does return, there will be a general resurrection of all people; unbelievers will also be raised in their bodies. Unbelievers will then experience a second death (verse 14). At their first death they died physically; now, at their second death, they will be cast into a lake of fire, out of God's presence.

But the second death has no power over believers. They reign with Christ, now, throughout the church age, when they die, and for ever.

There is a special mention of those who are martyrs. In the West we do not have personal experience of martyrdoms. But from Stephen onwards, there have been many who have been put to death for following Christ. They deserve special mention and they get that here in this passage. In Hebrews (12:1) we read:

> Therefore, since we are surrounded by such a great cloud of witnesses, let us throw off everything that hinders and the sin that so easily entangles, and let us run with perseverance the race marked out for us.

Many Christians read these words as though the witnesses (or martyrs) somehow surround us in the air and cheer us on in our Christian life. A better way to understand these words is to recognize that we are surrounded by the martyrs and witnesses to God in history, and as we look at them, we are encouraged by their example to keep moving on in the Christian life. The cure for our little worries is to look at the martyrs for the faith. Where are they? They are reigning with Christ. The book of Revelation gives us the heavenly realities behind the visible world. Those who have lived for Christ and then died by martyrdom seem to have lost everything, but have in fact gained everything. They reign with Christ.

I have always seen it as a challenge in my ministry to excite people about heaven and glory. We are such earthbound creatures, taken up with our jobs, mortgages, exams and holidays. The Bible does not teach us to have *no* concern about these things, but it does tell us that there is always the bigger picture. What happens when Christians die? They go to heaven, but more than that: they reign with Christ.

The Bible is concerned with every area of our life – singleness, family life, marriage, employment and many others – and is therefore a practical book. We need to take all the instruction we can from the word of God. But however well we manage our lives, there is still a bigger picture, which we will all one day see: – we will reign with Christ.

The end of Satan

We have already seen that the Beast is given considerable attention in Revelation, though more commonly we tend to use the term "the Antichrist". There is always a spirit of Antichrist at work in the world. This spirit is self-exalting, and demonstrates vitriolic opposition to the church; this opposition is often seen in cruel dictatorships. The Bible teaches all this, and that evil comes to a head at the end of history in the great tribulation, when enormous pressure will rise against the church. We have seen that several times in Revelation, but we read of it again in this chapter. The human face of opposition to the church is the Beast, but this chapter concentrates on the satanic power behind the Beast. When the thousand years at the end of the church age are over, Satan will be released to deceive the nations.

The mention of Gog and Magog reflects the Old Testament picture of the surrounding nations attacking Israel (Ezekiel 38:2). But here the picture is broadened out. We see a coalition of forces from all over the earth attacking God's people – "the city he loves" (verse 9), which must represent the church.

Although the tribulation threatens the church, it does not destroy it. Those opposed to the church will even seem for a time to be successful, but all opposition will eventually fall. Here we have the total picture. All rebellion against Christ will be destroyed, because finally Satan will be destroyed as well. "And the devil, who deceived them, was thrown into the lake of burning sulphur, where the beast and the false prophet had been thrown. They will be tormented day and night for ever and ever" (verse 10). This describes, in the strongest language possible, everlasting, unending ages.

Once again, we can claim that Revelation is about the victory of God. God cannot have the victory unless evil is destroyed, and here we see that Satan is cast down for ever. God not only wins some battles. His triumph is total; the enemy is destroyed.

God, in his grace, gives us, in our present age, a view of the end of all things. We should certainly not ignore the book of Revelation when its message is: God wins.

We may be under pressure now, and things may get much tougher. But the Devil, the great deceiver, will be seen to have had his day. In a short time, he will be cast down; it's in the book!

The final judgement

One of the most sobering passages in the entire Bible must be the last section of Revelation 20. With the return of Christ we come to the end of this age and to the time of final judgement before the great white throne. The throne of the Lord is "great"; this speaks of God's majesty. The throne is "white"; this speaks of God's holiness.

We read, "Earth and sky fled from his presence" (verse 11), which some interpret as the annihilation of the present creation before the new heaven and earth are created. But two verses later we are told, "The sea gave up the dead that were in it"; this would be somewhat difficult if the earth had disappeared! Once again, symbolism is being used to heighten the drama of the occasion. On the Day of Judgement, to which all history is moving, the sight that will absorb all our interest will be the great white throne and the one who is seated on it. It will be so awesome that nothing else will be in focus – all else will seem to flee.

John says that he "saw the dead, great and small, standing before the throne" (verse 12). Who will be there? The answer is that everyone is destined to die once, and then comes judgement (Hebrews 9:27). No one can avoid death, and so we will all be there, great and small. Kings and queens, dictators, American presidents and British prime ministers will be there. Billy Graham will be there and the homeless beggars in your town will be there. You and I will be there too.

What happens next? The books are opened. There are different books: "the book of life" and the books that record our works. Everybody is in the books that keep account of our works, but only Christians are in the book of life. The books of works remind us that everyone will be judged according to what they have done, and so everyone will receive a different verdict on Judgement Day. Some unbelievers will receive more severe punishment than others because of what they have done. Some Christians will receive greater rewards than others because of what they have done.

But the other book is still more important. "If anyone's name was not found written in the book of life, he was thrown into the lake of fire" (verse 15). We live in a world where everyone expresses an opinion. Everyone has an opinion on death, judgement, heaven and hell. What we read in the Bible saves us from our own opinions. God's word says that there is a Day of Judgement to come, the result of which will be an eternity with Christ, or an eternity without Christ.

Revelation is an account of a vision given to John by God. We read what will happen when Jesus returns at the end of history. By the end of this age, every promise and prophecy of Scripture will be fulfilled. This is not my opinion; it is God's decision. We need to know that our name is in the book of life. Our submission to Christ's rule means that our name is there and that we will reign with him for ever.

We can sum up the chapter by saying that Satan's destruction is certain, God's victory will be total, and believers will reign with Christ. There will be a final Day of Judgement when all accounts will be settled. Even death itself will die, so that, in the age to come, nothing will mar the joy of those whose names are in the book of life.

CHAPTER NINETEEN

THE NEW JERUSALEM
Revelation 21

There is a sense of progress in the book of Revelation. Following on from the Day of Judgement in the previous chapter, what we see in the last two chapters of the book is a description of the eternal age.

We are now able to view three things that are new:

● The new heaven and earth
● The new Jerusalem
● The new order

The new heaven and earth

"Then I saw a new heaven and a new earth, for the first heaven and the first earth had passed away, and there was no longer any sea" (verse 1).

This great statement proclaims that all biblical prophecy is now fulfilled. In the Old Testament, God promised new heavens and a new earth that would endure (Isaiah 66:22). Peter recalls this when he says, "But in keeping with his promise we are looking forward to a new heaven and a new earth, the home of righteousness" (2 Peter 3:13).

Opinions differ as to whether this means an entirely new

creation, or a total renewal of the present creation, although the majority view probably supports the latter. Certainly, Paul seems to suggest this when he speaks of the present creation as being subject to frustration but waiting for its liberation (Romans 8:20–21).

If we think of heaven in a vague and ethereal way, we will rob ourselves of the anticipation of something wonderful. Heaven should not be reduced to a cartoon image, where ghostlike figures sit on clouds playing harps. In fact, this section of Revelation corrects all such impoverished thinking, for we are given a truly robust view of the age to come. The new heaven and earth will be solid, real, renewed and restored to perfection. The earth will no longer be subject to pollution and decay. God will restore the whole of his creation under the headship of Jesus Christ in what the Bible calls "a new heaven and a new earth". What has been promised through the Scriptures John now sees. The ultimate plans of God are implemented, and so all biblical prophecy is fulfilled.

A question is often raised about the lack of any sea (verse 1). The sea seems to get a bad press in Revelation; as we have already seen, the Beast arises out of the sea (13:1). However, the sea was often thought of as something which separated people. So it would make sense if, instead of "no longer any sea", we read, "no longer any separation". In the new creation, there will be no more hindrances, barriers or dividing walls. Everything will be reunited under the headship of Christ.

In the age to come we will be given new resurrection bodies and will be part of a new creation, on a new earth. Think of the beauty of the present creation, spoiled though it is. We cannot begin to imagine the wonders of the age to come, the new heaven and the new earth that will be eternal.

The new Jerusalem

We now turn to the church in this eternal age. The primary theme of Revelation 21 is the church, pictured as the new Jerusalem. "I saw the Holy City, the new Jerusalem, coming down out of heaven from God, prepared as a bride beautifully dressed for her husband" (verse 2). John picks up this theme and develops it in detail from verse 9 to the end of the chapter. This allows us to observe some key truths about the church. We need to note that these verses are relevant also in describing our hopes and vision for the church in the present age. The church, even now, should reflect some characteristics of the church in the age to come.

The church is a city (verse 2)

Jerusalem, the city of God, the place where God lives, is a picture of the people of God throughout the Bible. Here, however, it seems to be a more complex picture, for the city is dressed as a bride. It would be a ridiculous picture if we were unable to identify the church as the bride of Christ. However, we know that this identification is correct, because in Revelation 19 we have already seen the church described as the bride at the wedding supper of the Lamb.

This picture warns us against a mistake that is frequently made: that of understanding the description of the city as a description of heaven. Quite commonly, heaven is thought of as something like a city, or even as an actual city. This is clearly wrong, because the city is dressed like a bride. We know that this bride is the church, so the city is also the church. This is a picture to teach us truths about the church, not to teach us what heaven looks like.

In the eternal age, the church does not *live* in the city; it *is* the city, the new Jerusalem.

It is also important that we should see the church as a city even now. Together we are a place of refuge for people seeking hope and safety. We are also a people built together. "Jerusalem is built like a city that is closely compacted together." (Psalm 122:3). This is a vision of community, the best expression of life in a city.

The city comes to earth

"And he carried me away in the Spirit to a mountain great and high, and showed me the Holy City, Jerusalem, coming down out of heaven from God" (verse 10). This descent of Jerusalem repeats what has already been described in verse 2. This, too, counters vague ideas of heaven; in the new creation the church descends. This means that in the new creation, as the church descends from heaven to earth, earth will become heaven. I have never been convinced that the church will occupy only a new earth when we are told that the whole of creation will be restored. Why is the universe so vast? Well, it may be that it is big enough for people who will live for ever – for the church in eternity. We will live on a new earth, where the wonders of the restored universe will be ours to explore for eternity.

However, for now, the church should be a colony of heaven upon the earth: full of joy, peace, praise and overwhelming love.

God will be in the city

"And I heard a loud voice from the throne saying, 'Now the dwelling of God is with men, and he will live with them. They will be his people, and God himself will be with them and be their God'" (verse 3). So God is in this city. Between the church and God there will be unhindered, unbroken fellowship for ever. God will live among us. The "dwelling of God with men" actually refers to God pitching his tent among us. This reflects the tabernacle in the desert when God lived among his people in the time of Moses. But it also reminds us of the incarnation: "The Word became flesh and made his dwelling among us" (John 1:14). So God, in all his grace and glory, who dwelt among his people in the desert, who was manifest from time to time in the history of his chosen people, and who was revealed to the eyes of faith in his incarnate Son, will finally be revealed for all to see.

Just imagine: wherever you look, God will be there. The sweetest moments spent with God on this earth will be a pale shadow compared to the joy we will experience without end. At the very end of his prophecy, Ezekiel says, "And the name of that city from that time on will be: THE LORD IS THERE" (48:35). When we consider the church on earth, what we should want above all else is that the Lord should be there. The church I belong to took the opportunity to change its name when it moved into a new building. Deciding on a new name proved to be a very demanding exercise (we eventually chose "The Church of Christ the King'); but the name that every church should have is: "THE LORD IS THERE."

The city will shine with glory

We read of the city, "It shone with the glory of God, and its brilliance was like that of a very precious jewel" (verse 11). This shining glory will be the result of God living with his church. If God is among us now, we too will shine with the glory of God.

I once visited Plymouth, on the east coast of America, where the Pilgrim Fathers, having escaped from persecution in this country, landed from the *Mayflower* in 1620. This area of the United States also knew revival during the ministry of Jonathan Edwards and the visits of Whitfield and Wesley in the late 1700s. My wife and I found, as far as we could judge from the noticeboard outside, what seemed to be an evangelical church to attend on the Sunday of our visit. After an opening hymn, the person giving the notices gave details of a church-members' meeting to follow the main service, for the purpose of discussing some alterations to the church building. Discussion, then disagreement arose from members of the congregation, as different individuals began to comment on the suitability and time of the meeting, whether there would be a quorum present and other points of order. All this took place in the main Sunday meeting of an evangelical church in the city where the Pilgrim Fathers had landed, and in New England with its history of revival. It was difficult not to feel sad, and to long: Lord, send us your glory.

The city will be vast

"The city was laid out like a square, as long as it was wide. He [the angel] measured the city with the rod and found it to be 12,000 stadia in length, and as wide and high as it is long" (verse 16). This verse might again tempt us to think of heaven in terms of a literal city in which the church lives – 1,400 miles long and 1,400 miles wide. However, the city as described is actually cubic, for it is also 1,400 miles high. This should therefore not be taken to be a literal city; rather, once again, something is being said about the church. The church in glory will be vast. In Revelation 7:9 it is described as "a great multitude that no-one could count". In eternity we will be amazed at the huge number of the redeemed. Stories of individual conversions can be very moving. What will also stir us in heaven will be the colossal scale of the work of redemption.

This should make us long to see the church grow in our own time. Churches may start small, but they should long to grow. Large churches should long to be bigger still. The church where I am a member, and one of the pastors, is a community of approximately 1,000 people. In British terms we are a big church. But it frustrates the leadership of our church that we are too small – we want to be bigger!

The church will be beautiful

This chapter goes on to describe the city walls, decorated with twelve kinds of precious stone. It speaks of the beauty of the church in eternity. What makes the church beautiful today? It is the members of the church functioning together in love. That makes the church shine with beauty on the earth.

The city will be holy

We are assured that nothing impure will ever enter the city (verse 27). The church will be for ever a holy city set apart for a holy God. In the days in which we live, we need to battle for our purity, as a people totally devoted to this holy God.

There are thus seven aspects of the church in eternity, but why must we wait for eternity? Of course, only in eternity will the church reach full perfection, but our yearning is that we should have more of the *then* right *now*. One of the angels carries John away to show him "the bride, the wife of the Lamb" (verse 9). Clearly, the angels take pride in the eternal city of God. It would be good to think that angels could look at our own church with pride and exclaim, "What a wonderful city!"

The new order

"He who was seated on the throne said, 'I am making everything new!'" (verse 5). What does that mean? The previous verse tells us, "He will wipe every tear from their eyes. There will be no more death or mourning or crying or pain, for the old order of things has passed away" (verse 4). Politicians are always speaking of a new order, especially if their party comes to power. But we know that one day there really will be a totally new order.

Do we believe that everything will be perfect one day, with no more pain, sickness, tears or death? Yes, we do, because he who sits on the throne says, "I am making everything new!" And the Alpha and the Omega says, "It is done" (verse 6). What great plans God has! All of them will be implemented and fulfilled. John has seen the city – he has seen the new heaven and earth – he has seen the new order.

Every biblical prophecy will be fulfilled.

CHAPTER TWENTY

PARADISE REGAINED
Revelation 22

We are now not simply at the end of the book of Revelation, but right at the end of the Bible. We tend to take note of last words. Here is God's last word, and it is a word that we should take note of. We read here of the blessings of eternity, and that Jesus is coming soon.

The blessings of eternity

In the previous chapter, the main emphasis was on the church in eternity. The church is the city of God, the new Jerusalem. Heaven is not a city; it is a new creation, a new heaven and new earth, and is the environment for the city of God. The church is not *in* the city of God; the church *is* the city of God. We read here of the blessings of the city of God in eternity.

It is paradise regained

Right at the beginning, God created paradise for humankind. He planted a garden; it was very beautiful, full of trees and fruitful. The tree of life was planted there, and a river flowed through. The picture given is one of total delight. Human beings were meant to enjoy paradise and were created for it. That is the beginning of the Bible. The rest of the Bible can be summarized as describing what went wrong and how God acted as a result. We read of that throughout the Bible, until, in the very last chapter of Revelation, we see that paradise is regained. We are back where we were meant to be. It is important to understand that the Bible is not a random collection of 66 books. It is essentially one book, telling one big story spanning the ages, from paradise lost to paradise regained.

Once again we read, in Revelation 22:1-2, of a river flowing; this is the river of the water of life. There is the tree of life, on each side of the river, producing fruit every month. This clearly symbolizes the fact that eternal fruitfulness from God will eternally exist throughout the city.

We may find it strange to read that the leaves of the tree are for the healing of the nations. Why would we need healing in eternity? Of course, this is again symbolic language; it is a reminder that no sickness will ever enter the city of God. At present, even in the body of Christ, there is a great deal of physical, mental and emotional sickness. We pray, we support individuals, we do see some healings, but a great deal of sickness remains. In this chapter, however, we see the blessings of eternity for the church. There will be no more sickness.

The river of the water of life flowing from the throne of God recalls a vision of the prophet Ezekiel. He saw a river flowing from the temple of God. "Swarms of living creatures will live wherever the river flows. There will be large numbers of fish, because this water flows there and makes the salt water fresh; so where the river flows everything will live" (Ezekiel 47:9). The river brings life. The good news is that this river of God does not only flow in Paradise regained; it flows now. Jesus said, "If anyone is thirsty, let him come to me and drink. Whoever believes in me, as the Scripture has said, streams of living water will flow from within him." John adds, "By this he meant the Spirit" (John 7:37-39). The river of God is the Holy Spirit within us. Any view that denies the experience of the Holy Spirit in a believer's life will rob us of the taste of paradise. When we know the flow of the river of God, when we experience the rush of the Spirit, then there is something of heaven in our soul.

The curse is lifted

"No longer will there be any curse" (verse 3). These are descriptions of the blessings of God in the eternal age. What shall we enjoy as the city of God? No longer will there be a curse. Once again, we read right at the beginning of the Bible that human sin brought a curse on everything. As a result, women give birth in pain, and harvesting the ground involves a battle against weeds and the elements. Life itself means for many that hard work will be necessary just for survival. Finally, there is death. But in paradise regained there will be no curse, no pain, no weeds, no exhausting work, and no death. The curse is lifted for the citizens of the city of God.

That does not mean that we will be doing nothing in heaven. Very often on a gravestone, we read "R.I.P." – or "Rest In Peace". Is that all we will do in eternity – simply rest in peace for ever? On the contrary, there will be plenty for us to do! In the original paradise, Adam was given responsibility for looking after the earth and naming the animals. There must be something equivalent to that in paradise regained: "No longer will there be any curse. The throne of God and of the Lamb will be in the city, and his servants will serve him" (verse 3). There will be no more curse; instead, we will serve the Lord. This tells us that work will lose all sense of drudgery. We may have known times when we have woken up in the morning with the thought, "Wonderful – work!" However, it has to be said that such times are not the norm! But in heaven, we will find work perpetually fascinating and refreshing. We will all be heavenly "workaholics"!

However, the word translated as "serve" can also be translated as "worship", and it is true that the highest level of service is worship. I have certainly enjoyed times of worship at a Bible Week, or in a service on a Sunday, when there has been such a sense of God's presence that I have wondered for a moment whether I am in heaven or on earth! That gives us some idea of what the service of God will be like; we will be caught up with

God, able to express our love, captivated afresh for all eternity by the glory of redemption, and adoring for ever the Lamb upon the throne. The curse will be lifted, and, unhindered by any constraints, we will be free to worship the living God.

The vision of God

"They will see his face, and his name will be on their foreheads" (verse 4).

The church is the city of God, but what will the church do in eternity? She will see the face of God. This is the pinnacle of Christian experience and privilege. One day, believers will see the face of God. There have previously been times when people have seen God, but not his face. In Exodus 24:9–10 we read of a group of elders of Israel who saw God, but not his face. Even that was enough to trigger a celebration. In Exodus 33, Moses daringly prays to God, "Now show me your glory" (verse 18). God then hides Moses in a cleft in the rock, and his glory passes by; but Moses only glimpses the back of God. However, one day we will see his face. One look upon the face of God would be enough to slay a mortal human being. But Revelation tells us that we will see his face. And God will look on our faces and see his name on our foreheads, which is surely the seal of God spoken of in chapter 7. There will be a face-to-face encounter, and God will know that we are his.

I travel by plane quite often. At the end of a journey, as you walk through the airport exit, what you look for is a face. It is such a pleasure to see a face that you know, waiting to welcome you. We will end this journey of life by seeing the face of God!

Revelation

"There will be no more night" (verse 5).

One of the remarkable features of being a Christian is what we now know. We are people of revelation. We know where we are from, our purpose for living, and where we are going. We even know that the world will end with the triumphant return of Jesus Christ. We know the answer to death and God's ultimate purpose for the creation. Our knowledge is amazing!

But there is even more that we do not know. There are many things that are unclear at the present time; we cannot grasp all the ways of God with our puny minds. We read that God, rather than the sun or moon, will give the city its light. That does not only mean that the city of God will be ablaze with the glory of God, but that everything will become clear in the light of God. "Now we see but a poor reflection as in a mirror; then we shall see face to face. Now I know in part; then I shall know fully, even as I am fully known" (1 Corinthians 13:12). In eternity, there will be no more darkness and no more confusion; everything will be in the light. All of God's truth will be clearly revealed. Verse 5 could imply that there will no longer be a sun or moon, but the emphasis is on the reality that whatever lights do shine will be outshone by the greater light of the glory of God. There will be no shadows in the city of God, for his glory and revelation will give us all the light that we will, or can, ever need.

An everlasting reign

"And they will reign for ever and ever" (verse 5b).

The idea that his disciples would reign in heaven is also implied in what Jesus taught in the gospels (Matthew 19:28). Revelation expands this. Reigning denotes authority. Jesus spoke of his disciples sitting on thrones and judging the tribes of Israel. Paul tells us that we shall judge the world and angels (1 Corinthians 6:2–3). We are going to reign and exercise authority. We do not know the detailed outworking of this, but it does remind us of the huge privilege of being the children of God.

The world in general thinks of people as "somebodies" and "nobodies". The "somebodies" are prominent in the media. They have the money, the fame, the status and the privileges. Most people, the "nobodies", are unknown outside a very small circle. "But God chose the foolish things of the world to shame the wise; God chose the weak things of the world to shame the strong. He chose the lowly things of this world and the despised things – and the things that are not – to nullify the things that are" (1 Corinthians 1:27–28). God chose many slaves for himself in the first centuries of Christian history. But they will reign with Christ. God is choosing simple, illiterate people in places like southern Africa today, but one day they will reign with Christ. So the status and position we are given as Christians is mind-blowing. We are sons and daughters of God, heirs of God, joint heirs with Christ *and* we will reign for ever.

To be a Christian is an incredible privilege. We can complain of pressures now, even those that come to us because we are Christians, but "our light and momentary troubles are achieving for us an eternal glory that far outweighs them all" (2 Corinthians 4:17). We do not merely have to hang on grimly at the present time. We are in training for reigning. When it's tough, and we overcome; when we pray, and see a breakthrough; when we witness, and see a conversion; when we give generously, and God provides; then we are in training for everlasting reigning!

Unlike earthly political systems and governments, none of which last more than a short time, God's government will last for ever. We will reign with him through endless ages.

Jesus is coming soon

In the final section of this final chapter, John touches on a number of issues, but the consistently recurring theme is the return of Jesus.

"Behold, I am coming soon!" (verse 7). Then again, "Behold, I am coming soon! My reward is with me, and I will give to everyone according to what he has done" (verse 12). In this last verse, we have a reminder that when Jesus comes again he will be the judge of all people. The New Testament clearly teaches that everyone will receive a judgement of their works. Although, for believers, there can be no loss of salvation, there are rewards to be gained or lost reflecting our works in this life.

There is some debate on the meaning of verse 17: "The Spirit and the bride say, 'Come!' And let him who hears say, 'Come!' Whoever is thirsty, let him come; and whoever wishes, let him take the free gift of the water of life." The bride, we know, is the church. The Spirit is the Holy Spirit, who inspires the church. But are they saying, "Come!" to Christ, or "Come!" to people who are looking for God?

The majority opinion is that the invitation is to Christ, who has promised to come soon. This is followed by an invitation to those searching for God. For them the invitation is to come and enjoy the benefits of salvation. If Jesus keeps promising to come soon, then naturally the church, inspired by the Holy Spirit, will be crying out, "Come!", on the basis of that promise. I have heard it suggested that this must have the idea not of command but of polite entreaty. Personally, I think that it has more the idea of desperation!

"Come, Lord Jesus!" is always on our lips. We long for him to come to us, because his coming is always the answer. We may have programmes, structures, courses and strategies, all of which can help, but none of which is the answer. The coming of the Lord is the answer to all our needs. There is a wonderful story of an Anglican clergyman, William Haslam, who was converted during the preaching of one of his own sermons! Here is the account in his own words.

> I do not remember all I said, but I felt a wonderful light and joy coming into my soul, and I was beginning to see what the Pharisees did not. Whether it was something in my words, or my manner, or my look, I do not know; but all of a sudden a local preacher, who happened to be in the congregation, stood up, and putting up his arms, shouted in the Cornish manner, "The parson is converted! The parson is converted! Hallelujah!" (Haslam, William, *From Death to Life*, Adam Gordon, 1994, p. 48).

Just a short time later, Haslam was preaching to 3,000 people in the open air, when the Spirit fell on people with mighty power and hundreds simultaneously fell over and began to cry to God for mercy. We need the Lord to come to us in the same way. More than anything, we need the Lord to come to us. The Spirit and the bride say, "Come!"

But there is still more: the answer will be revealed when Christ comes again. Then Satan will be cast down. All sin will be over, there will be an end to pain, sadness will be dismissed, and suffering and death will themselves die. All of this will happen when Jesus comes again. That is *the answer*; so the Spirit and the bride say, "Come!"

We find this again in verse 20. "He who testifies to these things says, 'Yes, I am coming soon.'" If Jesus says, "I am coming soon", three times in the last verses of the Bible, my less than profound conclusion is that it must be "soon"!

However, we have to deal with what can seem like a very long delay when Jesus says, "soon". Peter deals directly with this issue (2 Peter 3:3–9). He says that the cynics will exclaim that everything continues as normal, so how can we take seriously the claim that Christ will return? He makes three specific points.

Judgement comes suddenly

Noah built an ark over a period of 100 years. Scoffers would have stated that there was no sign of rain! But suddenly the flood came and swept them all away. The return of Christ will also be sudden and unexpected for the cynics.

God and human beings live in different time frames

None of us experiences the passage of time identically. We should hardly be surprised therefore that God's reckoning of time is beyond our comprehension. Peter reminds us that, "With the Lord a day is like a thousand years, and a thousand years are like a day" (2 Peter 3:8). What seems like a delay to us is not so to God.

The apparent delay in Christ's return shows the mercy of God

"He is patient with you, not wanting anyone to perish, but everyone to come to repentance" (2 Peter 3:9). God's apparent delay is actually a sign of his grace in giving more time for people to repent.

Jesus says he is coming soon. The world is cynical about such a claim, and the church must be careful not to take on the prevailing worldview. Jesus will soon return.

The very last verse of the Bible reads, "The grace of the Lord Jesus be with God's people. Amen" (verse 21).

Really, the last word is "grace". Past grace speaks of redemption accomplished for us. Present grace is enjoyed in the daily experiences of God's continual blessing on our lives. Future grace will be demonstrated in Christ's certain return.

From paradise lost to paradise regained through the work of Christ.

What a story!

What a gospel!

Jesus the Lamb triumphs!

The book of Revelation is a powerful declaration of the ultimate victory of God.

"Hallelujah! For our Lord God Almighty reigns."

BIBLIOGRAPHY

W. Barclay, *The Revelation of John, vols. 1 & 2* (Edinburgh: Saint Andrew Press, 1965).

G. K. Beale, *The Book of Revelation* (Grand Rapids: Eerdmans, 1999).

G. R. Beasley-Murray, *The Book of Revelation* (Oliphants, 1978).

G. B. Caird, *The Revelation of St John the Divine* (A & C Black, 1966).

W. Hendrikson, *More Than Conquerors* (London: Tyndale Press, 1962).

H. Hoeksema, *Behold He Cometh* (Reformed Free Publishing Association, 1986).

P. E. Hughes, *The Book of Revelation* (Leicester: IVP, 1990).

R. H. Mounce, *The Book of Revelation* (Grand Rapids: Eerdmans, 1998).

D. T. Niles, *As Seeing the Invisible* (London: SCM Press, 1964).

D. Pawson, *When Jesus Returns* (London: Hodder & Stoughton, 1995).

M. Wilcock, *The Message of Revelation* (Leicester: IVP, 1975).